Marxist Introductions

General Editor
Steven Lukes

Raymond Williams was formerly Professor of Drama and Fellow of Jesus College, Cambridge. His publications include *Culture and Society*, *Communications*, *The Country and The City*, and *Keywords*.

Marxism and Literature

RAYMOND WILLIAMS

Oxford   New York

OXFORD UNIVERSITY PRESS

Oxford University Press, Walton Street, Oxford OX2 6DP

Oxford New York
Athens Auckland Bangkok Bombay
Calcutta Cape Town Dar es Salaam Delhi
Florence Hong Kong Istanbul Karachi
Kuala Lumpur Madras Madrid Melbourne
Mexico City Nairobi Paris Singapore
Taipei Tokyo Toronto

and associated companies in
Berlin Ibadan

Oxford is a trade mark of Oxford University Press

British Library Cataloguing in Publication Data
Data available

Library of Congress Cataloging in Publication Data
Williams, Raymond.
Marxism and literature.—(Marxist introductions)
1. Communication and literature
I. Title. II. Series.
801 PN51
ISBN 0-19-876061-2

20 19 18 17 16 15

Printed in Great Britain by
Biddles Ltd
Guildford and King's Lynn

Contents

Introduction

This book is written in a time of radical change. Its subject, Marxism and Literature, is part of this change. Even twenty years ago, and especially in the English-speaking countries, it would have been possible to assume, on the one hand, that Marxism is a settled body of theory or doctrine, and, on the other hand, that Literature is a settled body of work, or kinds of work, with known general qualities and properties. A book of this kind might then reasonably have explored problems of the relations between them or, assuming a certain relationship, passed quickly to specific applications. The situation is now very different. Marxism, in many fields, and perhaps especially in cultural theory, has experienced at once a significant revival and a related openness and flexibility of theoretical development. Literature, meanwhile, for related reasons, has become problematic in quite new ways.

The purpose of this book is to introduce this period of active development, and to do so in the only way that seems appropriate to a body of thinking still in movement, by attempting at once to clarify and to contribute to it. This involves, necessarily, reviewing earlier positions, both Marxist and non-Marxist. But what is offered is not a summary; it is both a critique and an argument.

One way of making clear my sense of the situation from which this book begins is to describe, briefly, the development of my own position, in relation to Marxism and to literature, which, between them, in practice as much as in theory, have preoccupied most of my working life. My first contacts with Marxist literary argument occurred when I came to Cambridge to read English in 1939: not in the Faculty but in widespread student discussion. I was already relatively familiar with Marxist, or at least socialist and communist, political and economic analysis and argument. My experience of growing up in a working-class family had led me to accept the basic political position which they supported and clarified. The cultural and literary arguments, as I then encountered them, were in effect an extension from this, or a mode of affiliation to it. I did not then clearly realize this. The dependence, I believe, is still not generally realized, in its full implications. Hardly anyone becomes a Marxist for primarily cultural or literary reasons, but for compelling political and economic reasons. In the urgencies of the thirties or the seventies that is understandable, but it can mean that a style of thought and certain defining propositions are picked up and applied, in good faith, as part of a political commitment, without necessarily having much independent substance and indeed without necessarily following from the basic analysis and argument. This is how I would now describe my own position as a student between 1939 and 1941, in which a confident but highly selective Marxism co-existed, awkwardly, with my ordinary academic work, until the incompatibility — fairly easily negotiable as between students and what is seen as a teaching establishment — became a problem not for campaigns or polemics but, harshly enough, for myself and for anything that I could call my own thinking. What I really learned from, and shared with, the dominant tones of that English Marxist argument was what I would now call, still with respect, a radical populism. It was an active, committed, popular tendency, concerned rather more (and to its advantage) with making literature than with judging it, and concerned above all to relate active literature to the lives of the majority of our own people. At the same time, alongside this, its range even of Marxist ideas was relatively narrow, and there were many problems and kinds of argument, highly developed in specialized studies, with which it did not connect and which it could therefore often only dismiss. As the consequent difficulties emerged, in the areas of activity and interest with which I was most directly and personally concerned, I began sensing and defining a set of problems which have since occupied most of my work. Exceptionally isolated in the changing political and cultural formations of the later forties and early fifties, I tried to discover an area of studies in which some of these questions might be answered, and some even posed. At the same time I read more widely in Marxism, continuing to share most of its political and economic positions, but carrying on my own cultural and literary work and inquiry at a certain conscious distance. That period is summed up in my book *Culture and Society* and, in the present context, in its chapter on 'Marxism and Culture'.

But from the mid-fifties new formations were emerging, notably what came to be called the New Left. I found, at this time, an immediate affinity with my own kind of cultural and literary work (in positions which had in fact been latent as early as the work in *Politics and Letters* in 1947 and 1948; positions which remained undeveloped because the conditions for such a formation did not then fully exist). I found also, and crucially, Marxist thinking which was different, in some respects radically different, from what I and most people in Britain knew as Marxism. There was contact with older work that had not previously come our way— that of Lukács and of Brecht, for example. There was new contemporary work in Poland, in France, and in Britain itself. And while some of this work was exploring new ground, much of it, just as interestingly, was seeing Marxism as itself a historical development, with highly variable and even alternative positions.

I began then reading widely in the history of Marxism, trying especially to trace the particular formation, so decisive in cultural and literary analysis, which I now recognize as having been primarily systematized by Plekhanov, with much support from the later work of Engels, and popularized by dominant tendencies in Soviet Marxism. To see that theoretical formation clearly, and to trace its hybridization with a strong native radical populism, was to understand both my respect for and my distance from what I had hitherto known as Marxism *tout court*. It was also to gain a sense of the degree of selection and interpretation which, in relation both to Marx and to the whole long Marxist argument and inquiry, that familiar and orthodox position effectively represented. I could then read even the English Marxists of the thirties differently, and especially Christopher Caudwell. It is characteristic that the argument about Caudwell, which I had followed very carefully in the late forties and early fifties, had centred on the question characteristic of the style of that orthodox tradition: 'are his ideas Marxist or not?'. It is a style that has persisted, in some corners, with confident assertions that this or that is or is not a Marxist position. But now that I knew more of the history of Marxism, and of the variety of selective and alternative traditions within it, I could at last get free of the model which had been such an obstacle, whether in certainty or in doubt: the model of fixed and known Marxist positions, which in general had only to be applied, and the corresponding dismissal of all other kinds of thinking as non-Marxist, revisionist, neo-Hegelian, or bourgeois. Once the central body of thinking was itself seen as active, developing, unfinished, and persistently contentious, many of the questions were open again, and, as a matter of fact, my respect for the body of thinking as a whole, including the orthodox tradition now seen as a tendency within it, significantly and decisively increased. I have come to see more and more clearly its radical differences from other bodies of thinking, but at the same time its complex connections with them, and its many unresolved problems.

It was in this situation that I felt the excitement of contact with more new Marxist work: the later work of Lukács, the later work of Sartre, the developing work of Goldmann and of Althusser, the variable and developing syntheses of Marxism and some forms of structuralism. At the same time, within this significant new activity, there was further access to older work, notably that of the Frankfurt School (in its most significant period in the twenties and thirties) and especially the work of Walter Benjamin; the extraordinarily original work of Antonio Gramsci; and, as a decisive element of a new sense of the tradition, newly translated work of Marx and especially the *Grundrisse*. As all this came in, during the sixties and early seventies, I often reflected, and in Cambridge had direct cause to reflect, on the contrast between the situation of the socialist student of literature in 1940 and in 1970. More generally I had reason to reflect on the contrast for any student of literature, in a situation in which an argument that had drifted into deadlock, or into local and partial positions, in the late thirties and forties, was being vigorously and significantly reopened.

In the early seventies I began discussing these issues in lectures and classes in Cambridge: at first with some opposition from some of my Faculty colleagues, who knew (but did not know) what Marxism and Literature amounted to. But this mattered less than the fact that my own long and often internal and solitary debate with what I had known as Marxism now took its place in a serious and extending international inquiry. I had opportunities to extend my discussions in Italy, in Scandinavia, in France, in North America, and in Germany, and with visitors from Hungary, Yugoslavia, and the Soviet Union. This book is the result of that period of discussion, in an international context in which I have had the sense, for the first time in my life, of belonging to a sphere and dimension of *work* in which I could feel at home. But I have felt, at every point, the history of the previous thirty-five years, during which any contribution I might make had been developing in complex and in direct if often unrecorded contact, throughout, with Marxist ideas and arguments.

That individual history may be of some significance in relation to the development of Marxism and of thinking about Marxism in Britain during that period. But it has a more immediate relevance to the character of this book, and to its organization. In my first part I discuss and analyse four basic concepts: 'culture', 'language', 'literature', and 'ideology'. None of these is exclusively a Marxist concept, though Marxist thinking has contributed to them — at times significantly, in general unevenly. I examine specifically Marxist uses of the concepts, but I am concerned also to locate them within more general developments. This follows from the intellectual history I have described, in that I am concerned to see different forms of Marxist thinking as interactive with other forms of thinking, rather than as a separated history, either sacred or alien. At the same time, the re-examination of these fundamental concepts, and especially those of language and of literature, opens the way to the subsequent critique and contribution. In my second part I analyse and discuss the key concepts of Marxist cultural theory, on which — and this is an essential part of my argument — Marxist literary theory seems to me in practice to depend. It is not only an analysis of elements of a body of thinking; it explores significant variations and, at particular points and especially in its later chapters, introduces concepts of my own. In my third part, I again extend the discussion, into questions of literary theory, in which variants of Marxism are now interactive with other related and at times alternative kinds of thinking. In each part, while presenting analysis and discussion of key elements and variants of Marxist thinking, I am concerned also to develop a position which, as a matter of theory, I have arrived at over the years. This differs, at several key points, from what is most widely known as Marxist theory, and even from many of its variants. It is a position which can be briefly described as cultural materialism: a theory of the specificities of material cultural and literary production within historical materialism. Its details belong to the argument as a whole, but I must say, at this point, that it is, in my view, a Marxist theory, and indeed that in its specific fields it is, in spite of and even because of the relative unfamiliarity of some of its elements, part of what I at least see as the central thinking of Marxism.

To sustain analysis, discussion, and the presentation of new or modified theoretical positions, I have had to keep the book in a primarily theoretical dimension. In many quarters this will be well enough understood, and even welcomed. But I ought to say, knowing the strength of other styles of work, and in relation especially to many of my English readers, that while this book is almost wholly theoretical, every position in it was developed from the detailed practical work that I have previously undertaken, and from the consequent interaction with other, including implicit, modes of theoretical assumption and argument. I am perhaps more conscious than anyone of the need to give detailed examples to clarify some of the less familiar concepts, but, on the one hand, this book is intended as in some respects a starting-point for new work, and, on the other hand, some of the examples I would offer are already written in earlier books. Thus anyone who wants to know what I 'really, practically' mean by certain concepts can look, to take some leading instances, at the exemplification of signs and notations in *Drama in Performance*; of conventions in *Drama from Ibsen to Brecht*; of structures of feeling in *Modern Tragedy*, *The Country and the City*, and *The English Novel from Dickens to Lawrence*; of traditions, institutions, and formations, and of the dominant, the residual, and the emergent in parts of *Culture and Society* and in the second part of *The Long Revolution*; and of material cultural production in *Television: Technology and Cultural Form*. I would now write some of these examples differently, from a more developed theoretical position and with the advantage of a more extended and a more consistent vocabulary (the latter itself exemplified in *Keywords*). But the examples need to be mentioned, as a reminder that this book is not a separated work of theory; it is an argument based on what I have learned from all that previous work, set into a new and conscious relation with Marxism.

I am glad, finally, to be able to say how much I have learned from colleagues and students in many countries and especially in the University of Cambridge; in Stanford University, California; in McGill University, Montreal; in the Istituto Universitario Orientale, Naples; in the University of Bremen; and in the Institute for the Study of Cultural Development, Belgrade. I owe personal thanks to John Fekete and, over many years, to Edward Thompson and Stuart Hall. The book could not have been written without the unfailing co-operation and support of my wife.

R.W.

I. Basic Concepts

1. Culture

At the very centre of a major area of modern thought and practice, which it is habitually used to describe, is a concept, 'culture', which in itself, through variation and complication, embodies not only the issues but the contradictions through which it has developed. The concept at once fuses and confuses the radically different experiences and tendencies of its formation. It is then impossible to carry through any serious cultural analysis without reaching towards a consciousness of the concept itself: a consciousness that must be, as we shall see, historical. This hesitation, before what seems the richness of developed theory and the fullness of achieved practice, has the awkwardness, even the gaucherie, of any radical doubt. It is literally a moment of crisis: a jolt in experience, a break in the sense of history; forcing us back from so much that seemed positive and available — all the ready insertions into a crucial argument, all the accessible entries into immediate practice. Yet the insight cannot be sealed over. When the most basic concepts — the concepts, as it is said, from which we begin — are suddenly seen to be not concepts but problems, not analytic problems either but historical movements that are still unresolved, there is no sense in listening to their sonorous summons or their resounding clashes. We have only, if we can, to recover the substance from which their forms were cast.

Society, economy, culture: each of these 'areas', now tagged by a concept, is a comparatively recent historical formulation. 'Society' was active fellowship, company, 'common doing', before it became the description of a general system or order. 'Economy' was the management of a household and then the management of a community before it became the description of a perceived system of production, distribution, and exchange. 'Culture', before these transitions, was the growth and tending of crops and animals, and by extension the growth and tending of human faculties. In their modern development the three concepts did not move in step, but each, at a critical point, was affected by the movement of the others. At least this is how we may now see their history. But in the run of the real changes what was being put into the new ideas, and to some extent fixed in them, was an always complex and largely unprecedented experience. 'Society' with its received emphasis on immediate relationships was a conscious alternative to the formal rigidities of an inherited, then seen as an imposed, order: a 'state'. 'Economy', with its received emphasis on management, was a conscious attempt to understand and control a body of activities which had been taken not only as necessary but as given. Each concept then interacted with a changing history and experience. 'Society', chosen for its substance and immediacy, the 'civil society' which could be distinguished from the formal rigidities of 'state', became in its turn abstract and systematic. New descriptions became necessary for the immediate substance which 'society' eventually excluded. For example, 'individual', which had once meant indivisible, a member of a group, was developed to become not only a separate but an opposing term— 'the individual' and 'society'. In itself and in its derived and qualifying terms, 'society' is a formulation of the experience we now summarize as 'bourgeois society': its active creation, against the rigidities of the feudal 'state'; its problems and its limits, within this kind of creation, until it is paradoxically distinguished from and even opposed to its own initial impulses. Similarly, the rationality of 'economy', as a way of understanding and controlling a system of production, distribution, and exchange, in direct relation to the actual institution of a new kind of economic system, persisted but was limited by the very problems it confronted. The very product of rational institution and control was projected as 'natural', a 'natural economy', with laws like the laws of the ('unchanging') physical world.

Most modern social thought begins from these concepts, with the inherent marks of their formation and their unresolved problems usually taken for granted. There is then 'political', 'social' or 'sociological', and 'economic' thought, and these are believed to describe 'areas', perceived entities. It is then usually added, though sometimes reluctantly, that there are of course other 'areas': notably the 'psychological' and the 'cultural'. But while it is better to admit these than neglect them, it is usually not seen that their forms follow, in practice, from the unresolved problems of the initial shaping concepts. Is 'psychology' 'individual' ('psychological') or 'social'? That problem can be left for dispute within the appropriate discipline, until it is noticed that it is the problem of what is 'social' that the dominant development of 'society' has left unresolved. Are we to understand 'culture' as 'the arts', as 'a system of meanings and values', or as a 'whole way of life', and how are these to be related to 'society' and 'the economy'? The questions have to be asked, but we are unlikely to be able to answer them unless we recognize the problems which were inherent in the concepts 'society' and 'economy' and which have been passed on to concepts like 'culture' by the abstraction and limitation of those terms.

The concept of 'culture', when it is seen in the broad context of historical development, exerts a strong pressure against the limited terms of all the other concepts. That is always its advantage; it is always also the source of its difficulties, both in definition and comprehension. Until the eighteenth century it was still a noun of process: the culture *of* something—crops, animals, minds. The decisive changes in 'society' and 'economy' had begun earlier, in the late sixteenth and seventeenth centuries; much of their essential development was complete before 'culture' came to include its new and elusive meanings. These cannot be understood unless we realize what had happened to 'society' and 'economy'; but equally none can be fully understood unless we examine a decisive modern concept which by the eighteenth century needed a new word—*civilization*.

The notion of 'civilizing', as bringing men within a social organization, was of course already known; it rested on *civis* and *civitas*, and its aim was expressed in the adjective 'civil' as orderly, educated, or polite. It was positively extended, as we have seen, in the concept of 'civil society'. But 'civilization' was to mean more than this. It expressed two senses which were historically linked: an achieved state, which could be contrasted with 'barbarism', but now also an achieved state *of* development, which implied historical process and progress. This was the new historical rationality of the Enlightenment, in fact combined with a self-referring celebration of an achieved condition of refinement and order. It was this combination that was to be problematic. The developmental perspective of the characteristic eighteenth-century Universal History was of course a significant advance. It was the crucial step beyond the relatively static ('timeless') conception of history which had depended on religious or metaphysical assumptions. Men had made their own history, in this special sense: that they (or some of them) had achieved 'civilization'. This process was secular and developmental, and in that sense historical. But at the same time it was a history that had culminated in an achieved state: in practice the metropolitan civilization of England and France. The insistent rationality which explored and informed all the stages and difficulties of this process came to an effective stop at the point where civilization could be said to have been achieved. Indeed all that could be rationally projected was the extension and triumph of these achieved values.

This position, already under heavy attack from older religious and metaphysical systems and their associated notions of order, became vulnerable in new ways. The two decisive responses of a modern kind were, first, the idea of culture, offering a different sense of human growth and development, and, second, the idea of socialism, offering a social and historical criticism of and alternative to 'civilization' and 'civil society' as fixed and achieved conditions. The extensions, transfers, and overlaps between all these shaping modern concepts, and between them and residual concepts of much older kinds, have been quite exceptionally complex.

'Civilization' and 'culture' (especially in its common early form as 'cultivation') were in effect, in the late eighteenth century, interchangeable terms. Each carried the problematic double sense of an achieved state and of an achieved state of development. Their eventual divergence has several causes. First, there was the attack on 'civilization' as superficial; an 'artificial' as distinct from a 'natural' state; a cultivation of 'external' properties—politeness and luxury—as against more 'human' needs and impulses. This attack, from Rousseau on through the Romantic movement, was the basis of one important alternative sense of 'culture'—as a process of 'inner' or 'spiritual' as distinct from 'external' development. The primary effect of this alternative was to associate culture with religion, art, the family and personal life, as distinct from or actually opposed to 'civilization' or 'society' in its new abstract and general sense. It was from this sense, though not always with its full implications, that 'culture' as a general process of 'inner' development was extended to include a descriptive sense of the means and works of such development: that is, 'culture' as a general classification of 'the arts', religion, and the institutions and practices of meanings and values. Its relations with 'society' were then problematic, for these were evidently 'social' institutions and practices but were seen as distinct from the aggregate of general and 'external' institutions and practices now commonly called 'society'. The difficulty was ordinarily negotiated by relating 'culture', even where it was evidently social in practice, to the 'inner life' in its most accessible, secular forms: 'subjectivity', 'the imagination', and in these terms 'the individual'. The religious emphasis weakened, and was replaced by what was in effect a metaphysics of subjectivity and the imaginative process. 'Culture', or more specifically 'art' and 'literature' (themselves newly generalized and abstracted), were seen as the deepest record, the deepest impulse, and the deepest resource of the 'human spirit'. 'Culture' was then at once the secularization and the liberalization of earlier metaphysical forms. Its agencies and processes were distinctively human, and were generalized as subjective, but certain quasi-metaphysical forms—'the imagination', 'creativity', 'inspiration', 'the aesthetic', and the new positive sense of 'myth'—were in effect composed into a new pantheon.

This original break had been with 'civilization' in its assumed 'external' sense. But as secularization and liberalization continued, there was a related pressure on the concept of 'civilization' itself. This reached a critical point during the rapid development of industrial society and its prolonged social and political conflicts. In one view this process was part of the continuing development of civilization: a new and higher social order. But in another view civilization was the achieved state which these new developments were threatening to destroy. 'Civilization' then became an ambiguous term, denoting on the one hand enlightened and progressive development and on the other hand an achieved and threatened state, becoming increasingly retrospective and often in practice identified with the received glories of the past. In the latter sense 'civilization' and 'culture' again overlapped, as received states rather than as continuing processes. Thus, a new battery of forces was ranged against both culture and civilization: materialism, commercialism, democracy, socialism.

Yet 'culture', meanwhile, underwent yet another development.This is especially difficult to trace but is centrally important, since it led to 'culture' as a social—indeed specifically anthropological and sociological—concept. The tension and interaction between this developing sense and the other sense of 'inner' process and 'the arts' remain evident and important.

There was always, in practice, some connection between the two developments, though the emphases came to be very different. The origin of this second sense is rooted in the ambiguity of 'civilization' as both an achieved state and an achieved state of development. What were the properties of this achieved state and correspondingly the agencies of its development? In the perspective of the Universal Histories the characteristic central property and agency was reason—an enlightened comprehension of ourselves and the world, which allows us to create higher forms of social and natural order, overcoming ignorance and superstition and the social and political forms to which they have led and which they support. History, in this sense, was the progressive establishment of more rational and therefore more civilized systems. Much of the confidence of this movement was drawn from the enlightenment embodied in the new physical sciences, as well as from the sense of an achieved social order. It is very difficult to distinguish this new secular sense of 'civilization' from a comparably secular sense of 'culture' as an interpretation of human development. Each was a modern idea in the sense that it stressed human capacity not only to understand but to build a human social order. This was the decisive difference of both ideas from the earlier derivation of social concepts and social orders from presumed religious or metaphysical states. But when it came to identifying the real motive forces, in this secular process of 'man making his own history', there were radical differences of view.

Thus one of the very earliest emphases on 'man making his own history' was that of Vico, in The New Science (from 1725). He asserted

a truth beyond all question: that the world of civil society has certainly been made by men, and that its principles are therefore to be found within the modifications of our own human mind. Whoever reflects on this cannot but marvel that the philosophers should have bent all their energies to the study of the world of nature, which, since God made it, He alone knows; and that they should have neglected the study of the world of nations or civil world, which, since men had made it, men could hope to know. (p. 331)*

* All references are to editions specified in the Booklist.

Here, against the grain of the time, the 'natural sciences' are rejected but the 'human sciences' given a startling new emphasis. We can know what we have made, indeed know by the fact of making. The specific interpretations which Vico then offered are now of little interest, but his description of a mode of development which was at once, and interactively, the shaping of societies and the shaping of human minds is probably the effective origin of the general social sense of 'culture'. The concept itself was remarkably advanced by Herder, in *Ideas on the Philosophy of the History of Mankind* (1784–91). He accepted the emphasis on the historical self-development of humanity, but argued that this was much too complex to be reduced to the evolution of a single principle, and especially to something so abstract as 'reason'; and, further, that it was much too variable to be reduced to a pro-gressive unilinear development culminating in 'European civilization'. It was necessary, he argued, to speak of 'cultures' rather than 'culture', so as to acknowledge variability, and within any culture to recognize the complexity and variabi-lity of its shaping forces. The specific interpretations he then offered, in terms of 'organic' peoples and nations, and against the 'external universalism' of the Enlightenment, are elements of the Romantic movement and now of little active interest. But the idea of a fundamental social process which shapes speci-fic and distinct 'ways of life' is the effective origin of the *comparative* social sense of 'culture' and its now necessary plural 'cultures'.

The complexity of the concept of 'culture' is then remarkable. It became a noun of 'inner' process, specialized to its presumed agencies in 'intellectual life' and 'the arts'. It became also a noun of general process, specialized to its presumed configurations in 'whole ways of life'. It played a crucial role in definitions of 'the arts' and 'the humanities', from the first sense. It played an equally crucial role in definitions of the 'human sciences' and the 'social sciences', in the second sense. Each tendency is ready to deny any proper use of the concept to the other, in spite of many attempts at reconciliation. In any modern theory of cul-ture, but perhaps especially in a Marxist theory, this complexity is a source of great difficulty. The problem of knowing, at the outset, whether this would be a theory of 'the arts and intellec-tual life' in their relations to 'society', or a theory of the social process which creates specific and different 'ways of life', is only the most obvious problem.

The first substantial problem is in attitudes towards 'civilization'. Here the decisive intervention of Marxism was the analysis of 'civil society', and what within its terms was known as 'civilization', as a specific historical form: bourgeois society as created by the capitalist mode of production. This provided an indispensable critical perspective, but it was still largely contained within the assumptions which had produced the concept: that of a progressive secular development, most obviously; but also that of a broadly unilinear development. Bourgeois society and capitalist production were at once heavily attacked and seen as historically progressive (the latter in received terms, as in "the bourgeoisie ... has made barbarian and semi-barbarian countries dependent on the civilized ones", *Communist Manifesto*, 53). Socialism would supersede them as the next and highest stage of the development.

It is important to compare this inherited perspective with other elements in Marxism and in the radical and socialist movements which preceded it. Often, especially in the earlier movements, influenced by an alternative tradition, including the radical critique of 'civilization', it was not the progressive but the fundamentally contradictory character of this development that was decisive. 'Civilization' had produced not only wealth, order, and refinement, but as part of the same process poverty, disorder, and degradation. It was attacked for its 'artificiality—its glaring contrasts with a 'natural' or 'human' order. The values upheld against it were not those of the next higher stage of development, but of an essential human brotherhood, often expressed as something to be recovered as well as gained. These two tendencies in Marxism, and in the wider socialist movement, have often in effect been brought together, but in theory and especially in the analysis of subsequent historical practice need to be radically distinguished.

The next decisive intervention of Marxism was the rejection of what Marx called 'idealist historiography', and in that sense of the theoretical procedures of the Enlightenment. History was not seen (or not always or primarily seen) as the overcoming of ignorance and superstition by knowledge and reason. What that account and perspective excluded was material history, the history of labour, industry as the 'open book of the human faculties'. The original notion of 'man making his own history' was given a new radical content by this emphasis on 'man making himself' through producing his own means of life. For all its difficulties in detailed demonstration this was the most important intellectual advance in all modern social thought. It offered the possibility of overcoming the dichotomy between 'society' and 'nature', and of discovering new constitutive relationships between 'society' and 'economy'. As a specification of the basic element of the social process of culture it was a recovery of the wholeness of history. It inaugurated the decisive inclusion of that material history which had been excluded from the 'so-called history of civilization, which is all a history of religions and states'. Marx's own history of capitalism is only the most eminent example.

But there are difficulties within this achievement. Its emphasis on social process, of a constitutive kind, was qualified by the persistence of an earlier kind of rationalism, related to the assumption of progressive unilinear development, as in one version of the discovery of the 'scientific laws' of society. This weakened the constitutive and strengthened a more instrumental perspective. Again, the stress on material history, especially within the necessary polemics of its establishment, was in one special way compromised. Instead of making cultural history material, which was the next radical move, it was made dependent, secondary, 'superstructural': a realm of 'mere' ideas, beliefs, arts, customs, determined by the basic material history. What matters here is not only the element of reduction; it is the reproduction, in an altered form, of the separation of 'culture' from material social life, which had been the dominant tendency in idealist cultural thought. Thus the full possibilities of the concept of culture as a constitutive social process, creating specific and different 'ways of life', which could have been remarkably deepened by the emphasis on a material social process, were for a long time missed, and were often in practice superseded by an abstracting unilinear universalism. At the same time the significance of the alternative concept of culture, defining 'intellectual life' and 'the arts', was compromised by its apparent reduction to 'superstructural' status, and was left to be developed by those who, in the very process of idealizing it, broke its necessary connections with society and history and, in the areas of psychology, art, and belief, developed a powerful alternative sense of the constitutive human process itself. It is then not surprising that in the twentieth century this alternative sense has come to overlay and stifle Marxism, with some warrant in its most obvious errors, but without having to face the real challenge which was implicit, and so nearly clarified, in the original Marxist intervention.

In the complex development of the concept of 'culture', which has of course now been incorporated into so many different systems and practices, there is one decisive question which was returned to again and again in the formative period of the eighteenth and early nineteenth centuries but which was on the whole missed, or at least not developed, in the first stage of Marxism. This is the question of human language, which was an understandable preoccupation of the historians of 'civilization', and a central, even a defining question, for the theorists of a constitutive process of 'culture', from Vico to Herder and beyond. Indeed, to understand the full implications of the idea of a 'constitutive human process' it is to changing concepts of language that we must turn.

2. Language

A definition of language is always, implicitly or explicitly, a definition of human beings in the world. The received major categories—'world', 'reality', 'nature,' 'human'—may be counterposed or related to the category 'language', but it is now a commonplace to observe that all categories, including the category 'language', are themselves constructions in language, and can thus only with an effort, and within a particular system of thought, be separated from language for relational inquiry. Such efforts and such systems, nevertheless, constitute a major part of the history of thought. Many of the problems which have emerged from this history are relevant to Marxism, and in certain areas Marxism itself has contributed to them, by extension from its basic revaluation, in historical materialism, of the received major categories. Yet it is significant that, by comparison, Marxism has contributed very little to thinking about language itself. The result has been either that limited and undeveloped versions of language as a 'reflection' of 'reality' have been taken for granted, or that propositions about language, developed within or in the forms of other and often antagonistic systems of thought, have been synthesized with Marxist propositions about other kinds of activity, in ways which are not only ultimately untenable but, in our own time, radically limiting to the strength of the social propositions. The effects on cultural theory, and in particular on thinking about literature, have been especially marked.

The key moments which should be of interest to Marxism, in the development of thinking about language, are, first, the emphasis on language as *activity* and, second, the emphasis on the history of language. Neither of these positions, on its own, is enough to restate the whole problem. It is the conjunction and consequent revaluation of each position that remains necessary. But in different ways, and with significant practical results, each position transformed those habitual conceptions of language which depended on and supported relatively static ways of thinking about human beings in the world.

The major emphasis on language as activity began in the eighteenth century, in close relation to the idea of men having made their own society, which we have seen as a central element in the new concept of 'culture'. In the previously dominant tradition, through all its variations, 'language' and 'reality' had been decisively separated, so that philosophical inquiry was from the beginning an inquiry into the connections between these apparently separate orders. The pre-Socratic unity of the *logos*, in which language was seen as at one with the order of the world and of nature, with divine and human law, and with reason, had been decisively broken and in effect forgotten. The radical distinction between 'language' and 'reality', as between 'consciousness' and 'the material world', corresponding to actual and practical divisions between 'mental' and 'physical' activity, had become so habitual that serious attention seemed naturally concentrated on the exceptionally complicated consequent relations and connections. Plato's major inquiry into language (in the *Cratylus*) was centred on the problem of the correctness of *naming*, in which the interrelation of 'word' and 'thing' can be seen to originate either in 'nature' or in 'convention'. Plato's solution was in effect the foundation of idealist thought: there is an intermediate but constitutive realm, which is neither 'word' nor 'thing' but 'form', 'essence', or 'idea'. The investigation of either 'language' or 'reality' was then always, at root, an investigation of these constitutive (metaphysical) forms.

Yet, given this basic assumption, far-reaching inquiries into the uses of language could be undertaken in particular and specialized ways. Language as a way of indicating reality could be studied as *logic*. Language as an accessible segment of reality, especially in its fixed forms in writing, could be studied as *grammar*, in the sense of its formal and 'external' shape. Finally, within the distinction between language and reality, language could be conceived as an *instrument* used by men for specific and distinguishable purposes, and these could be studied in *rhetoric* and in the associated *poetics*. Through prolonged academic and scholastic development, these three great branches of language study—*logic*, *grammar*, and *rhetoric*—though formally associated in the medieval trivium, became specific and eventually separated disciplines. Thus though they made major practical advances, they either foreclosed examination of the form of the basic distinction between 'language' and 'reality', or determined the grounds, and especially the terms, in which such an examination might be made.

This is notably the case with the important medieval concept of sign, which has been so remarkably readopted in modern linguistic thought. 'Sign', from Latin *signum*, a mark or token, is intrinsically a concept based on a distinction between 'language' and 'reality'. It is an interposition between 'word' and 'thing' which repeats the Platonic interposition of 'form', 'essence', or 'idea', but now in accessible linguistic terms. Thus in Buridan 'natural signs' are the universal mental counterparts of reality and these are matched, by convention, with the 'artificial signs' which are physical sounds or letters. Given this starting-point, important investigations of the activity of language (but not of language as an activity) could be undertaken: for example, the remarkable speculative grammars of medieval thought, in which the power of sentences and of the modes of construction which underlay and complicated simple empirical notions of 'naming' was described and investigated. Meanwhile, however, the *trivium* itself, and especially grammar and rhetoric, moved into relatively formal, though immensely learned, demonstrations of the properties of a given body of 'classical' written material. What was later to be known as 'literary study', and from the early seventeenth century as 'criticism', developed from this powerful, prestigious, and limited mode.

Yet the whole question of the distinction between 'language' and 'reality' was eventually forced into consciousness, initially in a surprising way. Descartes, in reinforcing the distinction and making it more precise, and in demanding that the criterion of connection should be not metaphysical or conventional but grounded in scientific knowledge, provoked new questions by the very force of his scepticism about the old answers. It was in response to Descartes that Vico proposed his criterion that we can have full knowledge only of what we can ourselves make or do. In one decisive respect this response was reactionary. Since men have not in any obvious sense made the physical world, a powerful new conception of scientific knowledge was ruled out *a priori* and was, as before, reserved to God. Yet on the other hand, by insisting that we can understand society because we have made it, indeed that we understand it not abstractly but in the very process of making it, and that the activity of language is central in this process, Vico opened a whole new dimension.

It was and is difficult to grasp this dimension, initially

because Vico embedded it in what can be read as a schematic account of the stages of language development: the notorious three stages of divine, heroic, and human. Rousseau, repeating these three stages as 'historical' and interpreting them as stages of declining vigour, gave a form of argument to the Romantic Movement—the revival of literature as a revival of the 'original', 'primal' power of language. But this at once obscured the newly active sense of history (specializing it to regeneration and ultimately, as this failed, to reaction) and the newly active sense of language, which in being specialized to literature could be marked off as a special case, a special entity, a special function, leaving the 'non-literary' relations of language to reality as conventional and as alienated as before. To take Vico's three stages literally, or indeed as 'stages' at all, is to lose sight, as he did, of the dimension he had opened. For what was crucial, in his account of language, was that it emerged only at the human stage, the divine being that of mute ceremonies and rituals and the heroic that of gestures and signs. Verbal language is then distinctively human; indeed, constitutively human. This was the point taken up by Herder, who opposed any notion of language being 'given' to man (as by God) and, in effect, the apparently alternative notion of language being 'added' to man, as a special kind of acquisition or tool. Language is then, positively, a distinctively human opening of and opening to the world: not a distinguishable or instrumental but a constitutive faculty.

Historically this emphasis on language as constitutive, like the closely related emphasis on human development as culture, must be seen as an attempt both to preserve some idea of the generally human, in face of the analytical and empirical procedures of a powerfully developing natural science, and to assert an idea of human creativity, in face of the increased understanding of the properties of the physical world, and of consequently causal explanations from them. As such this whole tendency was in constant danger of becoming simply a new kind of idealism—'humanity' and 'creativity' being projected as essences—while the tendencies it opposed moved towards a new kind of objective materialism. This specific fission, so fateful in all subsequent thought, was in effect masked and ratified by a newly conventional distinction between 'art' (literature)—the sphere of 'humanity' and 'creativity'—and 'science' ('positive knowledge')—the knowable dimension of the physical world and of physical human beings within it. Each of the key terms—'art', 'literature', and 'science', together with the associated 'culture' and with such a newly necessary specialization as 'aesthetic' and the radical distinction between 'experience' and 'experiment'—changed in meaning between the early eighteenth and early nineteenth centuries. The resulting conflicts and confusions were severe, but it is significant that in the new situation of the nineteenth century the issues were never really joined on the ground of language, at any radical level, though it was precisely in relation to language that the newly conventional distinctions most needed to be challenged.

What happened instead was an extraordinary advance in empirical knowledge of languages, and a wholly remarkable analysis and classification of this knowledge in terms which set some of the basic questions aside. It is impossible to separate this movement from its political history, within the dynamic development of Western societies in a period of extending colonialism. Older studies of language had been largely contained within the model of the dead 'classical' languages (which still effectively determined 'grammar' in both its syntactic and literary senses) and of the 'derived' modern vernaculars. European exploration and colonization, meanwhile, had been dramatically expanding the available range of linguistic material. The critical encounter was between the European and Indian civilizations: not only in available languages but in European contact with the highly developed methods of Indic grammatical scholars, with their alternative body of 'classical' texts. It was as an Englishman in India that William Jones learned Sanskrit and from an observation of its resemblances to Latin and Greek began the work which led to classification of the Indo-European (Aryan) and other 'families' of languages.

This work, based on comparative analysis and classification, was procedurally very close to the evolutionary biology with which it is contemporary. It is one of the major periods of all scholarly investigation, empirically founding not only the major classifications of language families, including schemes of their evolutionary development and relationships, but also, within these schemes, discovering certain 'laws' of change, notably of sound-change. In one area this movement was 'evolutionary' in a particular sense: in its postulate of a proto-language (proto-Indo-European) from which the major 'family' had developed.

But in its later stages it was 'evolutionary' also in another sense. Increasing rigour in the study of sound-changes associated one branch of language study with natural science, so that a system of linguistic phonetics marched with physical studies of the language faculty and the evolutionary origins of speech. This tendency culminated in major work in the physiology of speech and in the field significantly designated within this area as experimental psychology.

This identification of language-use as a problem in psychology was to have major effects on concepts of language. But meanwhile within general language-studies there was a new phase which reinforced inherent tendencies to objectivism. What was characteristically studied in comparative philology was a body of records of language: in effect, centrally, the alien written word. This assumption of the defining material of study was already present, of course, in the earlier phase of 'classical' language studies: Greek, Latin, Hebrew. But then the modes of access to a wider range of languages repeated this earlier stance: that of the privileged (scientific) observer of a body of alien written material. Methodological decisions, substantially similar to those being developed in the closely related new science of anthropology, followed from this effective situation. On the one hand there was the highly productive application of modes of systematic observation, classification, and analysis. On the other hand there was the largely unnoticed consequence of the privileged situation of the observer: that he was observing (of course scientifically) within a differential mode of contact with alien material: in texts, the records of a past history; in speech, the activity of an alien people in subordinate (colonialist) relations to the whole activity of the dominant people within which the observer gained his privilege. This defining situation inevitably reduced any sense of language as actively and presently constitutive. The consequent objectivism of fundamental procedure was intensely productive at the level of description, but necessarily any consequent definition of language had to be a definition of a (specialized) philological system. In a later phase of this contact between privileged observer and alien language material, in the special circumstances of North America where hundreds of native American (Amerindian) languages were in danger of dying out after the completion of European conquest and domination, the earlier philological procedures were

indeed, characteristically, found to be not objective enough.
Assimilation of these even more alien languages to the
categories of Indo-European philology—the natural reflex of
cultural imperialism—was scientifically resisted and checked
by necessary procedures which, assuming only the presence of
an alien system, found ways of studying it in its own (intrinsic
and structural) terms. This approach was a further gain in scientific description, with its own remarkable results, but at the level
of theory it was the final reinforcement of a concept of language
as an (alien) objective system.

Paradoxically, this approach had even deeper effect through
one of the necessary corrections of procedure which followed
from the new phase of contact with languages without texts.
Earlier procedures had been determined by the fact that a language almost invariably presented itself in specific past texts:
finished monologic utterances. Actual speech, even when it was
available, was seen as derived, either historically into vernaculars, or practically into speech acts which were instances of the
fundamental (textual) forms of the language. Language-use
could then hardly ever be seen as itself active and constitutive.
And this was reinforced by the political relations of the
observer–observed, where the 'language-habits' studied, over a
range from the speech of conquered and dominated peoples to
the 'dialects' of outlying or socially inferior groups, theoretically matched against the observer's 'standard', were regarded
as at most 'behaviour', rather than independent, creative, self-
directing life. North American empirical linguistics reversed
one part of this tendency, restoring the primacy of speech in the
literal absence of 'standard' or 'classical' texts. Yet the objectivist character of the underlying general theory came to limit
even this, by converting speech itself to a 'text'—the characteristically persistent word in orthodox structural linguistics. Language came to be seen as a fixed, objective, and in these senses
'given' system, which had theoretical and practical priority over
what were described as 'utterances' (later as 'performance').
Thus the living speech of human beings in their specific social
relationships in the world was theoretically reduced to
instances and examples of a system which lay beyond them.

The major theoretical expression of this reified understanding
of language came in the twentieth century, in the work of Saussure, which has close affinities to the objectivist sociology of

Durkheim. In Saussure the social nature of language is expressed as a system (*langue*), which is at once stable and autonomous and founded in normatively identical forms; its 'utterances' (*paroles*) are then seen as 'individual' (in abstract distinction from 'social') uses of 'a particular language code' through an enabling 'psycho-physical mechanism'. The practical results of this profound theoretical development, in all its phases, have been exceptionally productive and striking. The great body of philological scholarship has been complemented by a remarkable body of linguistic studies, in which the controlling concept of language as a formal system has opened the way to penetrating descriptions of actual language operations and many of their underlying 'laws'.

This achievement has an ironic relation with Marxism. On the one hand it repeats an important and often dominant tendency within Marxism itself, over a range from the comparative analysis and classification of stages of a society, through the discovery of certain fundamental laws of change within these systematic stages, to the assertion of a controlling 'social' system which is *a priori* inaccessible to 'individual' acts of will and intelligence. This apparent affinity explains the attempted synthesis of Marxism and structural linguistics which has been so influential a phenomenon of the mid-twentieth century. But Marxists have then to notice, first, that history, in its most specific, active, and connecting senses, has disappeared (in one tendency has been theoretically excluded) from this account of so central a social activity as language; and second, that the categories in which this version of system has been developed are the familiar bourgeois categories in which an abstract separation and distinction between the 'individual' and the 'social' have become so habitual that they are taken as 'natural' starting-points.

In fact there was little specifically Marxist work on language before the twentieth century. In their chapter on Feuerbach in *The German Ideology* Marx and Engels touched on the subject, as part of their influential argument against pure, directive consciousness. Recapitulating the 'moments' or 'aspects' of a materialist conception of history, they wrote:

Only now, after having considered four moments, four aspects of the fundamental historical relationships, do we find that man also posses-

ses 'consciousness'; but, even so, not inherent, not 'pure' consciousness. From the start the 'spirit' is afflicted with the curse of being
'burdened' with matter, which here makes its appearance in the form of
agitated layers of air, sounds, in short of language. Language is as old as
consciousness, language is practical consciousness, as it exists for other
men, and for that reason is really beginning to exist for me personally as
well; for language, like consciousness, only arises from the need, the
necessity, of intercourse with other men. (GI, 19)

So far as it goes, this account is wholly compatible with the
emphasis on language as practical, constitutive activity. The
difficulty arises, as it had also arisen in a different form in
previous accounts, when the idea of the constitutive is broken
down into elements which are then temporally ordered. Thus
there is an obvious danger, in the thinking of Vico and Herder, of
making language 'primary' and 'original', not in the acceptable
sense that it is a necessary part of the very act of human self-
creation, but in the related and available sense of language as *the*
founding element in humanity: "in the beginning was the
Word". It is precisely the sense of language as an *indissoluble*
element of human self-creation that gives any acceptable meaning to its description as 'constitutive'. To make it *precede all*
other connected activities is to claim something quite different.

The idea of language as constitutive is always in danger of this
kind of reduction. Not only, however, in the direction of the
isolated creative word, which becomes idealism, but also, as
actually happened, in objectivist materialism and positivism,
where 'the world' or 'reality' or 'social reality' is categorically
projected as the pre-existent formation to which language is
simply a response.

What Marx and Engels actually say, in this passage, points to
simultaneity and totality. The 'fundamental historical relationships' are seen as 'moments' or 'aspects', and man then 'also
possesses' consciousness'. Moreover, this language is material:
the "agitated layers of air, sounds", which are produced by the
physical body. It is then not a question of any temporal priority
of the 'production of material life' considered as a separable act.
The distinctively human mode of this primary material production has been characterized in three aspects: needs, new needs,
and human reproduction—"not of course to be taken as three
different stages . . . but . . . which have existed simultaneously
since the dawn of history and the first men, and still assert

themselves in history today". The distinctive humanity of the development is then expressed by the fourth 'aspect', that such production is *from the beginning also* a social relationship. It then involves from the beginning, as a necessary element, that practical consciousness which is language.

Thus far the emphasis is primarily 'constitutive', in the sense of an indissoluble totality of development. But it is easy to see how, in this direction also, what begins as a mode of analysis of aspects of a total process develops towards philosophical or 'natural' categories—simple materialist statements which retain the idealist separation of 'language' from 'reality' but simply reverse their priority—and towards historical categories, in which there is, *first*, material social production and *then* (rather than *also*) language.

In its predominantly positivist development, from the late nineteenth to the mid-twentieth century, a dominant kind of Marxism made this practical reduction: not so much directly in language theory, which on the whole was neglected, but habitually in its accounts of consciousness and in its analyses of the practical language activities which were grouped under the categories of 'ideology' and 'the superstructure'. Moreover this tendency was reinforced by the wrong kind of association with important scientific work on the physical means of language. This association was wholly compatible with an emphasis on language as material, but, given the practical separation of 'the world' and 'the language in which we speak about it', or in another form, of 'reality' and 'consciousness', the materiality of language could be grasped only as physical—a set of physical properties—and not as material *activity*: in fact the ordinary scientistic dissociation of the abstracted physical faculty from its actual human use. The resulting situation had been well described, in another context, by Marx, in the first 'thesis' on Feuerbach:

The chief defect of all materialism up to now (including Feuerbach's) is, that the object, reality, what we apprehend through our senses, is understood only in the form of the *object of contemplation* (*anschauung*); but not as *sensuous human activity*, as *practice*; not subjectively. Hence in opposition to materialism the *active* side was developed abstractly by idealism—which of course does not know real sensuous activity as such. (*GI*, 197)

This was indeed the situation in thinking about language. For the active emphases of Vico and Herder had meanwhile been remarkably developed, notably by Wilhelm von Humboldt. Here the inherited problem of the origin of language had been remarkably restated. Language of course developed at some point in evolutionary history, but it is not only that we have virtually no information about this; it is mainly that any human investigation of so constitutive an activity finds language already there in itself and in its presumed object of study. Language has then to be seen as a persistent kind of creation and re-creation: a dynamic presence and a constant regenerative process. But this emphasis, again, can move in different directions. It could reasonably have been associated with the emphasis of whole, indissoluble practice, in which the 'dynamic presence' and the 'constant regenerative process' would be necessary forms of the 'production and reproduction of real life' similarly conceived. What happened instead, in Humboldt and especially after him, was a projection of this idea of activity into essentially idealist and quasi-social forms: either the 'nation', based on an abstract version of the 'folk-mind' or the (ahistorical) 'collective consciousness'; or the 'collective spirit', the abstract creative capacity—self-creative but prior to and separate from material social practice, as in Hegel;, or, persuasively, the 'individual', abstracted and defined as 'creative subjectivity', the starting-point of meaning.

The influence of these various projections has been deep and prolonged. The abstract idea of the 'nation' could be readily connected with major philological work on the 'families' of languages and on the distinctive inherited properties of particular languages. The abstract idea of the 'individual' could be readily connected with the emphasis on a primary subjective reality and a consequent 'source' of meaning and creativity which emerged in the Romantic concepts of 'art' and 'literature' and which defined a major part of the development of 'psychology'.

Thus the stress on language as activity, which was the crucial contribution of this line of thinking, and which was a crucial correction of the inherent passivity, usually formalized in the metaphor of 'reflection', of positivism and objectivist materialism, was in turn reduced from specific activities (then necessarily social and material, or, in the full sense, historical) to *ideas* of such activity, categorized as 'nation' or 'spirit' or the 'creative individual'. It is significant that one of these categories, the 'individual' (not the specific, unique human being, who cannot of course be in doubt, but the generalization of the common property of all these beings as 'individuals' or 'subjects', which are already *social* categories, with immediate social implications), was prominent also within the dominant tendency of objectivist materialism. The exclusion of activity, of making, from the category of 'objective reality' left it contemplated only by 'subjects', who might in one version be ignored in the observation of objective reality – the active 'subject' replaced by the neutral 'observer'—or in another version, when it became necessary to speak about language or about other forms of practice, appeared in 'inter-subjective' relations—speaking to or at each other, passing information or a 'message' between each other, as separate or distinguishable identities, rather than ever *with* each other, the fact of language constituting and confirming their relationship. Language here decisively lost its definition as *constitutive* activity. It became a tool or an instrument or a medium taken up by individuals when they had something to communicate, as distinct from the faculty which made them, from the beginning, not only able to relate and communicate, but in real terms to be practically conscious and so to possess the active practice of language.

Against this reduction of language to instrumentality, the idea of language as expression, which was the main outcome of the idealist version of language as activity, was evidently attractive. It appeared literally to speak to an experience of language which the rival theory, confined to passing information, exchanging messages, naming objects, in effect suppressed. It could include the experience of speaking *with* others, of *participating* in language, of making and responding to rhythm or intonation which had no simple 'information' or 'message' or 'object' content: the experience, indeed, which was most evident in 'literature' and which was even, by specialization, made identical with it. Yet what actually happened was a deep split, which produced its own powerful categories of separation, some of them old terms in new forms: categorical divisions between the 'referential' and the 'emotive', between the 'denotative' and the 'connotative', between 'ordinary language' and 'literary language'. Certainly the uses towards which these categories point can be distinguished as the elements of specific practices, defined by specific situations. But their projection as categories, and then their further projection as separate entities, separate 'bodies' of language-use, permitted a dissolution and specialization which for a long time prevented the basic issues of the unfinished argument about language from becoming focused within a single area of discourse.

Marxism might have become this area of discourse, but it had developed its own forms of limitation and specialization. The most evident of these was a specialization of the whole material social process to 'labour', which was then more and more narrowly conceived. This had its effect in the important argument about the origins and development of language, which could have been reopened in the context of the new science of evolutionary physical anthropology. What happened instead was an application of the abstract concept of 'labour' as the single effective origin. Thus, in a modern authoritative account:

First labour, then articulate speech, were the two chief stimuli under the influence of which the brain of the ape gradualy changed into the human brain. (*Fundamentals of Dialectical Materialism*, ed. Schneierson, Moscow, 1967, 105)

This not only establishes an abstract, two-stage temporal development. It also converts both labour and language to 'stimuli', when the real emphasis should be on connected practice. This leads to an abstraction of evolutionary stages:

The development of labour brought the members of the community more closely together, for it enabled them to extend their joint activity and to support each other. Labour relations gave rise to the need for primitive men to speak and communicate with each other.

(Ibid. 105)

This is in effect an idealism of abstracted stimuli and needs. It must be contrasted with a properly materialist theory, in which labour and language, as practices, can be seen as evolutionarily and historically constitutive:

The argument that there could be no language without all the structure of modern man is precisely the same as the old theory that human hands made implement-making and using possible. But the implements are thousands of years older than hands of the modern human form. Modern speech-producing structures are the result of the evolutionary success of language, just as the uniquely human hand is the result of the evolutionary success of implements. (J. S. Washburn and J. B. Lancaster, *Current Anthropology*, vol. 12, No. 3, 1971)

Any constitutive theory of practice, and especially a materialist theory, has important effects beyond the question of origins, in restating the problem of the active process of language at any time: a restatement which goes beyond the separated categories of 'language' and 'reality'. Yet orthodox Marxism remained stuck in reflection theory, because this was the only plausible materialist connection between the received abstract categories. Reflection theory, in its first period, was itself specialized to crude stimulus-and-response models, adapted from positivist physiology. In its second period, in the later work of Pavlov, it added, as a way of dealing with the special properties of language, the concept of the 'second signal system', the first being the simple physical system of sensations and responses. This was better than nothing, but it assimilated language to the characteristics of a 'signal system', in relatively mechanistic ways, and was in practice unequal to problems of meaning beyond simple models of the associative. Setting out from this point, L.S. Vygotsky (*Thought and Language*, Moscow, 1934) proposed a new social theory, still named the 'second signal system', in which language and consciousness are freed from simple analogies with physical perception. His work on the development of language in children, and on the crucial problem of 'inner speech', provided a new starting-point, within a historical-materialist perspective. But for a generation, in orthodox Marxism, this was neglected. Meanwhile the work of N. S. Marr, based on older models, tied language to the 'superstructure' and even to simple class bases. Dogmatic positions, taken from other areas of Marxist thinking, limited the necessary theoretical developments. It is ironic that the influence of Marr was in effect ended by Stalin in 1950 with declarations that language was not 'part of the superstructure' and that languages did not have any essential 'class character' but rather a 'national character'. Ironic because though the declarations were necessary, in that context, they simply threw the argument back to a much earlier stage, in which the status of 'reflection' and, very specifically, the status of 'the superstructure', had, in Marxist terms, needed question. By this time, moreover, linguistics had come to be dominated by a specific and distinctive form of objectivism, which had produced the powerful systems of structuralism and semiotics. It was at this point that generally Marxist positions in other fields, especially in the popular form of objectively determined systems, were practically synthesized with theories of language which, from a fully Marxist position, needed to be profoundly opposed.

Such theories had been profoundly opposed in the 1920s in Leningrad, where the beginnings of a school of Marxist linguistics, of a significant kind, had in fact emerged. It is best represented by the work of V.N. Vološinov, whose *Marxism and the Philosophy of Language* appeared, in two editions, in 1929 and 1930; the second edition has been translated into English (Matejka and Titunik, New York and London, 1973). It is now widely believed that Vološinov was the pen-name of M.M. Bakhtin, author of a study of Dostoevsky (*Problemy Ivor cestva Dostoevskogo*, 1929; new version, with new title, *Problemy poetiki Dostoevskogo*, 1963); see also 'P.N. Medvedev' (author of *Formal'ny metod v literaturovedenii—kriticeskoe vvedenie v sociologiceskuju poètiku—The Formal Method in Literary Scholarship: a critical introduction to sociological poetics*—1928). However this may be, we can conveniently refer to the text published under that name as Vološinov.

Vološinov's decisive contribution was to find a way beyond the powerful but partial theories of expression and objective system. He found it in fundamentally Marxist terms, though he had to begin by saying that Marxist thinking about language was virtually non-existent. His originality lay in the fact that he did not seek to apply other Marxist ideas to language. On the contrary he reconsidered the whole problem of language within a general Marxist orientation. This enabled him to see 'activity' (the strength of the idealist emphasis after Humboldt) as social activity and to see 'system' (the strength of the new objectivist linguistics) in relation to this social activity and not, as had hitherto been the case, formally separated from it. Thus in drawing on the strengths of the alternative traditions, and in setting them side by side showing their connected radical weaknesses, he opened the way to a new kind of theory which had been necessary for more than a century.

Much of his effort went to recovering the full emphasis on language as activity, as practical consciousness, which had been weakened and in effect denied by its specialization to a closed

'individual consciousness' or 'inner psyche'. The strength of
this tradition was still its insistence on the active creation of
meanings, as distinct from the alternative assumption of a
closed formal system. Vološinov argued that meaning was
necessarily a social action, dependent on a social relationship.
But to understand this depended on recovering a full sense of
'social', as distinct both from the idealist reduction of the social
to an inherited, ready-made product, an 'inert crust', beyond
which all creativity was individual, and from the objectivist
projection of the social into a formal system, now autonomous
and governed only by its internal laws, within which, and solely
according to which, meanings were produced. Each sense, at
root, depends on the same error: of separating the social from
individual meaningful activity (though the rival positions then
valued the separated elements differently). Against the
psychologism of the idealist emphasis, Vološinov argued that
"consciousness takes shape and being in the material of signs
created by an organized group in the process of its social intercourse. The individual consciousness is nurtured on signs; it derives its growth from them; it reflects their logic and laws" (13).

Normally, it is at just this point (and the danger is always
increased by retaining the concept of 'sign', which Vološinov
revalued but continued to use) that objectivism finds its entry.
'The material of signs' can be translated as 'system of signs'. This
system can then be projected (by some notion of a theoretical
'social contract', as in Saussure, protected from examination by
the assumption of the priority of 'synchronic' over 'diachronic'
analysis) both beyond history and beyond any active conception
of contemporary social life, in which socially related individuals meaningfully participate, as distinct from acting out the laws
and codes of an inaccessible linguistic system. Each side of
Vološinov's argument has a continuing relevance, but it is in his
(incomplete) revaluation of the concept of 'sign' that his contemporary significance is most evident.

Vološinov accepted that a 'sign' in language has indeed a
'binary' character. (In fact, as we shall see, his retention of these
terms made it easier for the radical challenge of his work to be
missed.) That is to say, he agreed that the verbal sign is not
equivalent to, nor simply a reflection of, the object or quality
which it indicates or expresses. The relation within the sign
between the formal element and the meaning which this ele-

ment carries is thus inevitably conventional (thus far agreeing with orthodox semiotic theory), but it is not arbitrary* and, crucially, it is not fixed. On the contrary the fusion of formal element and meaning (and it is this fact of dynamic fusion which makes retention of the 'binary' description misleading) is the result of a real process of social development, in the actual activities of speech and in the continuing development of a language. Indeed signs can exist only when this active social relationship is posited. The usable sign—the fusion of formal element and meaning—is a product of this continuing speech-activity between real individuals who are in some continuing social relationship. The 'sign' is in this sense their product, but not simply their past product, as in the reified accounts of an 'always-given' language system. The real communicative 'products' which are usable signs are, on the contrary, living evidence of a continuing social process, into which individuals are born and within which they are shaped, but to which they then also actively contribute, in a continuing process. This is at once their socialization and their individuation: the connected aspects of a single process which the alternative theories of 'system' and 'expression' had divided and dissociated. We then find not a reified 'language' and 'society' but an active *social language*. Nor (to glance back at positivist and orthodox materialist theory) is this language a simple 'reflection' or 'expression' of 'material reality'. What we have, rather, is a grasping of this reality through language, which as practical consciousness is saturated by and saturates all social activity, including productive activity. And, since this grasping is social and continuous (as distinct from the abstract encounters of 'man' and 'his world', or 'consciousness' and 'reality', or 'language' and 'material existence'), it occurs within an active and changing society. It is of and to this experience—the lost middle term between the abstract entities, 'subject' and 'object', on which the propositions of idealism and orthodox materialism are erected—that language speaks. Or to put it more directly, language is the articulation of this active and changing experi-

---

* The question of whether a sign is 'arbitrary' is subject to some local confusion. The term was developed in distinction from the 'iconic', to indicate, correctly, that most verbal signs are not 'images' of things. But other senses of 'arbitrary', in the direction of 'random' or 'casual', had developed, and it was these that Vološinov opposed.

ence; a dynamic and articulated social *presence* in the world.

Yet it remains true that the mode of articulation is specific. This is the part of the truth which formalism had grasped. The articulation can be seen, and in some respects has to be seen, as both formal and systematic. A physical sound, like many other natural elements, may be made into a sign, but its distinction, Vološinov argued, is always evident: "a sign does not simply exist as part of a reality—it reflects and refracts another reality". What distinguishes it as a sign, indeed what made it a sign, is in this sense a formal process: a specific articulation of a meaning. Formalist linguistics had emphasized this point, but it had not discerned that the process of articulation is necessarily also a *material* process, and that the sign itself becomes part of a (socially created) physical and material world: "whether in sound, physical mass, colour, movement of the body or the like". Signification, the social creation of meanings through the use of formal signs, is then a practical material activity; it is indeed, literally, a means of production. It is a specific form of that practical consciousness which is inseparable from all social material activity. It is not, as formalism would make it, and as the idealist theory of expression had from the beginning assumed, an operation of and within 'consciousness', which then becomes a state or a process separated, *a priori*, from social material activity. It is, on the contrary, at once a distinctive material process—the making of *signs*—and, in the central quality of its distinctiveness as practical consciousness, is involved from the beginning in all other human social and material activity.

Formalist systems can appear to meet this point by referring it to the 'already-given', the 'last-instance determination of the economic structure', as in some current versions of structuralist Marxism. It is to avoid this kind of reduction that we must consider Vološinov's crucial distinction between a 'sign' and a 'signal'. In reflexive theories of language, whether positivist kinds of materialism, or such theories as psychological behaviourism, all 'signs' are in effect reduced to 'signals', within the simple models of 'object' and 'consciousness' or 'stimulus' and 'response'. Meanings are created by (repeated) recognition of what are then in effect 'signals': of the properties of an object or the character of a stimulus. 'Consciousness' and 'response' then 'contain' (for this is what meaning now is) those properties or that character. The assigned passivity and mechanism of such accounts have often been recognized. Indeed it was against such passivity and mechanism that formalism had most to contribute, in its insistence on the specific (formal) articulation of meanings through signs.

But it has been less often noticed that quite different theories, based on the determinate character of systems of signs, depend, ultimately, on a comparable idea of the fixed character of the sign, which is then in effect a displacement of fixed content to fixed form. Intense argument between these rival schools has allowed us to overlook the fact that the conversion of the 'sign' (as the term itself always made possible and even likely) into either fixed content or fixed form is a radical denial of active practical consciousness. The sign, in either case, is moved in the direction of a signal, which Vološinov distinguishes from a sign by the fact that it is intrinsically limited and invariant. The true quality of a sign (one would have preferred him to say, of a signifying element of a language) is that it is effective in communication, a genuine fusion of a formal element and a meaning (a quality that it indeed shares with signals); but also that as a function of continuing social activity it is capable of modification and development: the real processes that may be observed in the history of a language, but which the privileged priority of 'synchronic' analysis had ignored or reduced to a secondary or accidental character.

Indeed since it exists, as a sign, by its quality of signifying relationship—both the relation between formal element and meaning (its internal structure) and the relations between the people who in actually using it, in practical language, make it a sign—it has, like the social experience which is the principle of its formation, both dialectical and generative properties. Characteristically it does not, like a signal, have fixed, determinate, invariant meaning. It must have an effective nucleus of meaning but in practice it has a variable range, corresponding to the endless variety of situations within which it is actively used. These situations include new and changing as well as recurrent relationships, and this is the reality of the sign as dynamic fusion of 'formal element' and 'meaning'—'form' and 'content'—rather than as fixed, 'already-given' internal significance. This variable quality, which Vološinov calls *multi-accentual*, is of course the necessary challenge to the idea of 'correct' or 'proper' meanings, which had been powerfully developed by orthodox philology from its studies of dead languages, and which had been taken over both into social-class distinctions of a 'standard' language flanked either by 'dialects' or by 'errors', and into literary theories of a 'correct' or 'objective' reading. But the quality of variation—not random variation but variation as a necessary element of practical consciousness—bears heavily also against objectivist accounts of the sign-system. It is one of the decisive arguments against reduction of the key fact of social determination to the idea of determination by a system. But, while it thus bears heavily against all forms of abstract objectivism, it offers a basis also for a vital reconsideration of the problem of 'subjectivity'.

The signal, in its fixed invariance, is indeed a collective fact. It may be received and repeated, or a new signal may be invented, but in either case the level at which it operates is of a collective kind: that is to say, it has to be recognized but it need not be internalized, at that level of sociality which has excluded (as reductive versions of the 'social' commonly exclude) active participation by conscious individuals. The signal, in this sense, is fixed, exchangeable, collective property; characteristically it is easily both imported and exported. The true signifying element of language must from the beginning have a different capacity: to become an inner sign, part of an active practical consciousness. Thus in addition to its social and material existence between actual individuals, the sign is also part of a verbally constituted consciousness which allows individuals to use signs of their own initiative, whether in acts of social communication or in practices which, not being *manifestly* social, can be interpreted as personal or private.

This view is then radically opposed to the construction of all acts of communication from pre-determined objective relationships and properties, within which no individual initiative, of a creative or self-generating kind, would be possible. It is thus a decisive theoretical rejection of mechanical, behaviourist, or Saussurean versions of an objective system which is beyond individual initiative or creative use. But it is also a theoretical rejection of subjectivist theories of language as individual expression, since what is internally constituted is the social fact of the sign, bearing a definite though never fixed or invariant social meaning and relationship. Great strength has been given, and continues to be given, to theories of language as individual expression, by the rich practical experience of 'inner signs'—inner language—in repeated individual awareness of 'inner language activities', whether we call them 'thought' or 'consciousness' or actual verbal composition. These 'inner' activities involve the use of words which are not, at least at that stage, spoken or written to any other person. Any theory of language which excludes this experience, or which seeks to limit it to some residue or by-product or rehearsal (though it may often be these) of manifest social language activity, is again reductive of social language as practical consciousness. What has really to be said is that the sign is social but that in its very quality as sign it is capable both of being internalized—indeed has to be internalized, if it is to be a sign for communicative relation between actual persons, initially using only their own physical powers to express it—and of being continually available, in social and material ways, in manifest communication. This fundamental relationship between the 'inner' and the 'material' sign—a relationship often experienced as a tension but always lived as an activity, a practice—needs further radical exploration. In individual developmental psychology Vygotsky began this exploration, and at once discerned certain crucially distinguishing characteristics of 'inner speech', themselves constitutive rather than, as in Vološinov, merely transferred. This is still within the perspective of a historical materialist theory. The complex relationship, from another direction, needs specifically historical exploration, for it is in the movement from the production of language by human physical resources alone, through the material history of the production of other resources and of the problems of both technology and notation then involved in them, to the active social history of the complex of communicative systems which are now so important a part of the material productive process itself, that the dynamics of social language—its development of new means of production within a basic means of production—must be found.

Meanwhile, following Vološinov, we can see that just as all social process is activity between real individuals, so individuality, by the fully social fact of language (whether as 'outer' or 'inner' speech), is the active constitution, within distinct physical beings, of the social capacity which is the means of realization of any individual life. Consciousness, in this precise sense, is social being. It is the possession, through active and specific social development and relationships, of a precise social capacity, which is the 'sign-system'. Vološinov, even after these fundamental restatements, continues to speak of the 'sign-system': the formulation that had been decisively made in Saussurean linguistics. But if we follow his arguments we find how difficult and misleading this formulation can be. 'Sign' itself—the mark or token: the formal element—has to be revalued to emphasize its variability and internally active elements, indicating not only an internal structure but an internal dynamic. Similarly, 'system' has to be revalued to emphasize social process rather than fixed 'sociality': a revaluation that was in part made by Jakobson and Tynjanov (1928), within formalist argument, with the recognition that 'every system necessarily exists as an evolution while, on the other hand, evolution is inescapably of a systemic nature'. Although this was a necessary recognition, it was limited by its perspective of determinate systems within an 'evolutionary' category—the familiar reification of objective idealism—and still requires amendment by the full emphasis of social process. Here, as a matter of absolute priority, men relate and continue to relate before any system which is their product can as a matter of practical rather than abstract consciousness be grasped or exercise its determination.

These changes will have to be made, in the continuing inquiry into language. But the last point indicates a final difficulty. Much of the social process of the creation of meanings was projected within objectivist linguistics to the formal relations—thus the systematic nature—of signs. What at the level of the sign had been abstractly and statically conceived was set into a kind of motion—albeit a frozen, determinate motion, a movement of ice-fields—in the relational 'laws' or 'structures' of the system as a whole. This extension to a relational system, including its formal aspect as grammar, is in any case inevitable. Isolation of 'the sign', whether in Saussure or Vološinov, is at best an analytical procedure, at worst an evasion. Much of the important work on relations within a whole system is therefore an evident advance, and the problem of the variability of the sign can appear to be contained within the variability of its formal relations. But while this kind of emphasis on the relational system is obviously necessary, it is limited by the consequence of the initial abstract definition of the sign. The highly complex relations of (theoretically) invariable units can never be substantive relationships; they must remain as formal relationships. The internal dynamics of the sign, including its social and material relationships as well as its formal structure, must be seen as necessarily connected with the social and material as well as the formal dynamics of the system as a whole. There have been some advances in this direction in recent work (Rossi-Landi, 1975).

But there has also been a move which seems to reopen the whole problem. In Chomskyan linguistics there has been a decisive step towards a conception of system which emphasizes the possibility and the fact of individual initiative and creative practice which earlier objectivist systems had excluded. But at the same time this conception stresses deep structures of language formation which are certainly incompatible with ordinary social and historical accounts of the origin and development of language. An emphasis on deep constitutive structures, at an evolutionary rather than a historical level, can of course be reconciled with the view of language as a constitutive human faculty: exerting pressures and setting limits, in determinate ways, to human development itself. But while it is retained as an exclusively evolutionary process, it moves, necessarily, towards reified accounts of 'systemic evolution': development by constituted systems and structures (the constitution now at once permitting and limiting variations) rather than by actual human beings in a continuing social practice. Here Vygotsky's work on inner speech and consciousness is theoretically crucial:

If we compare the early development of speech and of intellect—which, as we have seen, develop along separate lines both in animals and in very young children—with the development of inner speech and of verbal thought, we must conclude that the later stage is not a simple continuation of the earlier. *The nature of the development itself changes, from biological to socio-historical*. Verbal thought is not an innate, natural form of behaviour but is determined by a historical-cultural process and has specific properties and laws that cannot be found in the natural forms of thought and speech. (*Thought and Language*, 51)

Thus we can add to the necessary definition of the biological faculty of language as *constitutive* an equally necessary definition of language development—at once individual and social—as historically and socially *constituting*. What we can then define is a dialectical process: the *changing practical con-*

sciousness of human beings, in which both the evolutionary and
the historical processes can be given full weight, but also within
which they can be distinguished, in the complex variations of
actual language use. It is from this theoretical foundation that
we can go on to distinguish 'literature', in a specific socio-
historical development of writing, from the abstract retrospective concept, so common in orthodox Marxism, which reduces
it, like language itself, to a function and then a (superstructural)
by-product of collective labour. But before we can go on to this,
we must examine the concepts of literature which, based on
earlier theories of language and consciousness, stand in the way.

3. Literature

It is relatively difficult to see 'literature' as a concept. In ordinary usage it appears to be no more than a specific description, and what is described is then, as a rule, so highly valued that there is a virtually immediate and unnoticed transfer of the specific values of particular works and kinds of work to what operates as a concept but is still firmly believed to be actual and practical. Indeed the special property of 'literature' as a concept is that it claims this kind of importance and priority, in the concrete achievements of many particular great works, as against the 'abstraction' and 'generality' of other concepts and of the kinds of practice which they, by contrast, define. Thus it is common to see 'literature' defined as 'full, central, immediate human experience', usually with an associated reference to 'minute particulars'. By contrast, 'society' is often seen as essentially general and abstract: the summaries and averages, rather than the direct substance of human living. Other related concepts, such as 'politics', 'sociology', or 'ideology', are similarly placed and downgraded, as mere hardened outer shells compared with the living experience of literature.

The naïvety of the concept, in this familiar form, can be shown in two ways: theoretically and historically. It is true that one popular version of the concept has been developed in ways that appear to protect it, and in practice do often protect it, against any such arguments. An essential abstraction of the 'personal' and the 'immediate' is carried so far that, within this highly developed form of thought, the whole process of abstraction has been dissolved. None of its steps can be retraced, and the abstraction of the 'concrete' is a perfect and virtually unbreakable circle. Arguments from theory or from history are simply evidence of the incurable abstraction and generality of those who are putting them forward. They can then be contemptuously rejected, often without specific reply, which would be only to fall to their level.

This is a powerful and often forbidding system of abstraction, in which the concept of 'literature' becomes actively ideological. Theory can do something against it, in the necessary recognition (which ought hardly, to those who are really in contact with literature, to need any long preparation) that whatever else 'it' may be, literature is the process and the result of formal composition within the social and formal properties of a language. The effective suppression of this process and its circumstances, which is achieved by shifting the concept to an undifferentiated equivalence with 'immediate living experience' (indeed, in some cases, to more than this, so that the actual lived experiences of society and history are seen as less particular and immediate than those of literature) is an extraordinary ideological feat. The very process that is specific, that of actual composition, has effectively disappeared or has been displaced to an internal and self-proving procedure in which writing of this kind is genuinely believed to be (however many questions are then begged) 'immediate living experience' itself. Appeals to the history of literature, over its immense and extraordinarily various range, from the *Mabinogion* to *Middlemarch*, or from *Paradise Lost* to *The Prelude*, cause a momentary hesitation until various dependent categories of the concept are moved into place: 'myth', 'romance', 'fiction', 'realist fiction', 'epic', 'lyric', 'autobiography'. What from another point of view might reasonably be taken as initial definitions of the processes and circumstances of composition are converted, within the ideological concept, to 'forms' of what is still triumphantly defined as 'full, central, immediate human experience'. Indeed when any concept has so profound and complex an internal specializing development, it can hardly be examined or questioned at all from outside. If we are to understand its significance, and the complicated facts it partially reveals and partially obscures, we must turn to examining the development of the concept itself.

In its modern form the concept of 'literature' did not emerge earlier than the eighteenth century and was not fully developed until the nineteenth century. Yet the conditions for its emergence had been developing since the Renaissance. The word itself came into English use in the fourteenth century, following French and Latin precedents; its root was Latin *littera*, a letter of the alphabet. *Litterature*, in the common early spelling, was then in effect a condition of reading: of being able to read and of having read. It was often close to the sense of modern *literacy*, which was not in the language until the late nineteenth century, its introduction in part made necessary by the movement of *literature* to a different sense. The normal adjective associated with literature was *literate*. *Literary* appeared in the sense of reading ability and experience in the seventeenth century, and did not acquire its specialized modern meaning until the eighteenth century.

Literature as a new category was then a specialization of the area formerly categorized as *rhetoric* and *grammar*: a specialization to reading and, in the material context of the development of printing, to the printed word and especially the book. It was eventually to become a more general category than *poetry* or the earlier *poesy*, which had been general terms for imaginative composition, but which in relation to the development of *literature* became predominantly specialized, from the seventeenth century, to metrical composition and especially written and printed metrical composition. But *literature* was never primarily the active composition—the 'making'—which *poetry* had described. As reading rather than writing, it was a category of a different kind. The characteristic use can be seen in Bacon—"learned in all literature and erudition, divine and humane"—and as late as Johnson—"he had probably more than common literature, as his son addresses him in one of his most elaborate Latin poems". *Literature*, that is to say, was a category of use and condition rather than of production. It was a particular specialization of what had hitherto been seen as an activity or practice, and a specialization, in the circumstances, which was inevitably made in terms of social class. In its first extended sense, beyond the bare sense of 'literacy', it was a definition of 'polite' or 'humane' learning, and thus specified a particular social distinction. New political concepts of the 'nation' and new valuations of the 'vernacular' interacted with a persistent emphasis on 'literature' as reading in the 'classical' languages. But still, in this first stage, into the eighteenth century, *literature* was primarily a generalized social concept, expressing a certain (minority) level of educational achievement. This carried with it a potential and eventually realized alternative definition of *literature* as 'printed books': the objects in and through which this achievement was demonstrated.

It is important that, within the terms of this development, literature normally included all printed books. There was not necessary specialization to 'imaginative' works. Literature was still primarily reading ability and reading experience, and this included philosophy, history, and essays as well as poems. Were the new eighteenth-century novels 'literature'? That question was first approached, not by definition of their mode or content, but by reference to the standards of 'polite' or 'humane' learning. Was drama literature? This question was to exercise successive generations, not because of any substantial difficulty but because of the practical limits of the category. If literature was reading, could a mode written for spoken performance be said to be literature, and if not, where was Shakespeare? (But of course he could *now* be read; this was made possible, and 'literary', by *texts*.)

At one level the definition indicated by this development has persisted. Literature lost its earliest sense of reading ability and reading experience, and became an apparently objective category of printed works of a certain quality. The concerns of a 'literary editor' or a 'literary supplement' would still be defined in this way. But three complicating tendencies can then be distinguished: first, a shift from 'learning' to 'taste' or 'sensibility' as a criterion defining literary quality; second, an increasing specialization of literature to 'creative' or 'imaginative' works; third, a development of the concept of 'tradition' within national terms, resulting in the more effective definition of 'a national literature'. The sources of each of these tendencies can be discerned from the Renaissance, but it was in the eighteenth and nineteenth centuries that they came through most powerfully, until they became, in the twentieth century, in effect received assumptions. We can look more closely at each tendency.

The shift from 'learning' to 'taste' or 'sensibility' was in effect the final stage of a shift from a para-national scholarly profession, with its original social base in the church and then in the universities, and with the classical languages as its shared material, to a profession increasingly defined by its class position, from which essentially general criteria, applicable in fields other than literature, were derived. In England certain specific features of bourgeois development strengthened the shift; the 'cultivated amateur' was one of its elements, but 'taste' and 'sensibility' were essentially unifying concepts, in class terms, and could be applied over a very wide range from public and private behaviour to (as Wordsworth complained) either wine or poetry. As subjective definitions of apparently objective criteria (which acquire their apparent objectivity from an actively consensual class sense), and at the same time apparently objective definitions of subjective qualities, 'taste' and 'sensibility' are characteristically bourgeois categories.

'Criticism' is an essentially associated concept, in the same development. As a new term, from the seventeenth century, it developed (always in difficult relations with its general and persistent sense of fault-finding) from 'commentaries' on literature, within the 'learned' criterion, to the conscious exercise of 'taste', 'sensibility', and 'discrimination'. It became a significant special form of the general tendency in the concept of literature towards an emphasis on the use or (conspicuous) consumption of works, rather than on their production. While the habits of use or consumption were still the criteria of a relatively integrated class, they had their characteristic strengths as well as weaknesses. 'Taste' in literature might be confused with 'taste' in everything else, but, within class terms, responses to literature were notably integrated, and the relative integration of the 'reading public' (a characteristic term of the definition) was a sound base for important literary production. The reliance on 'sensibility', as a special form of an attempted emphasis on whole 'human' response, had its evident weaknesses in its tendency to separate 'feeling' from 'thought' (with an associated vocabulary of 'subjective' and 'objective', 'unconscious' and 'conscious', 'private' and 'public'). At the same time it served, at its best, to insist on 'immediate' and 'living' substance (in which its contrast with the 'learned' tradition was especially marked). It was really only as this class lost its relative cohesion and dominance that the weakness of the concepts *as concepts* became evident. And it is evidence of at least its residual hegemony that *criticism*, taken as a new conscious discipline into the universities, to be practised by what became a new para-national profession, retained these founding class concepts, alongside attempts to establish new abstractly objective criteria. More seriously, criticism was taken to be a natural definition of literary studies, themselves defined by the specializing category (printed works of a certain quality) of *literature*. Thus these forms of the concepts of literature and criticism are, in the perspective of historical social development, forms of a class specialization and control of a general social practice, and of a class limitation of the questions which it might raise.

The process of the specialization of 'literature' to 'creative' or

'imaginative' works is very much more complicated. It is in part
a major affirmative response, in the name of an essentially general human 'creativity', to the socially repressive and intellectually mechanical forms of a new social order: that of capitalism
and especially industrial capitalism. The practical specialization of work to the wage-labour production of commodities; of
'being' to 'work' in these terms; of language to the passing of
'rational' or 'informative' 'messages'; of social relations to functions within a systematic economic and political order: all these
pressures and limits were challenged in the name of a full and
liberating 'imagination' or 'creativity'. The central Romantic
assertions, which depend on these concepts, have a significe-
antly absolute range, from politics and nature to work and art.
'Literature' acquired, in this period, a quite new resonance, but it
was not yet a specialized resonance. That came later as, against
the full pressures of an industrial capitalist order, the assertion
became defensive and reserving where it had once been positive
and absolute. In 'art' and 'literature', the essential and saving
human qualities must, in the early phase, be 'extended'; in the
later phase, 'preserved'.

Several concepts developed together. 'Art' was shifted from
its sense of a general human skill to a special province, defined
by 'imagination' and 'sensibility'. 'Aesthetic', in the same
period, shifted from its sense of general perception to a
specialized category of the 'artistic' and the 'beautiful'. 'Fiction'
and 'myth' (a new term from the early nineteenth century) might
be seen from the dominant class position as 'fancies' or 'lies' but
from this alternative position were honoured as the bearers of
'imaginative truth'. 'Romance' and 'romantic' were given newly
specialized positive emphases. 'Literature' moved with all
these. The wide general meaning was still available, but a
specialized meaning came steadily to predominate, around the
distinguishing qualities of the 'imaginative' and the 'aesthetic'.
'Taste' and 'sensibility' had begun as categories of a social condition. In the new specialization, comparable but more elevated
qualities were assigned to 'the works themselves', the 'aesthetic
objects'.

But there was still one substantial uncertainty: whether the
elevated qualities were to be assigned to the 'imaginative'
dimension (access to a truth 'higher' or 'deeper' than 'scientific'
or 'objective' or 'everyday' reality; a claim consciously substitut-

ing itself for the traditional claims of religion) or to the 'aesthe-tic' dimension ('beauties' of language or style). Within the specialization of literature, alternative schools made one or other of these emphases, but there were also repeated attempts to fuse them, making 'truth' and 'beauty', or 'truth' and 'vitality of language', identical. Under continuing pressure these argu-ments became not only positive assertions but increasingly negative and comparative, against all other modes: not only against 'science' and 'society'—the abstract and generalizing modes of other 'kinds' of experience—and not only against other kinds of writing—now in their turn specialized as 'discursive' or 'factual'—but, ironically, against much of 'literature' itself—'bad' writing, 'popular' writing, 'mass culture'. Thus the category which had appeared objective as 'all printed books', and which had been given a social-class foundation as 'polite learning' and the domain of 'taste' and 'sensibility', now became a necessarily selective and self-defining area: not all 'fiction' was 'imaginative'; not all 'literature' was 'Literature'. 'Criticism' acquired a quite new and effectively primary importance, since it was now the only way of validating this specialized and selective category. It was at once a discrimination of the authen-tic 'great' or 'major' works, with a consequent grading of 'minor' works and an effective exclusion of 'bad' or 'negligible' works, and a practical realization and communication of the 'major' values. What had been claimed for 'art' and the 'creative imagi-nation' in the central Romantic arguments was now claimed for 'criticism', as the central 'humane' activity and 'discipline'.

This development depended, in the first place, on an elabora-tion of the concept of 'tradition'. The idea of a 'national litera-ture' had been growing strongly since the Renaissance. It drew on all the positive forces of cultural nationalism and its real achievements. It brought with it a sense of the 'greatness' or 'glory' of the native language, for which before the Renaissance there had been conventional apology by comparison with a 'classical' range. Each of these rich and strong achievements had been actual; the 'national literature' and the 'major language' were now indeed 'there'. But, within the specialization of 'litera-ture', each was re-defined so that it could be brought to identity with the selective and self-defining 'literary values'. The 'national literature' soon ceased to be a history and became a tradition. It was not, even theoretically, all that had been written or all kinds of writing. It was a selection which culminated in, and in a circular way defined, the 'literary values' which 'criticism' was asserting. There were then always local disputes about who and what should be included, or as commonly excluded, in the definition of this 'tradition'. To have been an Englishman and to have written was by no means to belong to the 'English literary tradition', just as to be an Englishman and to speak was by no means to exemplify the 'greatness' of the language—indeed the practice of most English speakers was continually cited as 'ignorance' or 'betrayal' or 'debasement' of just this 'greatness'. Selectivity and self-definition, which were the evident processes of 'criticism' of this kind, were, however, projected as 'literature' itself, as 'literary values' and even finally as 'essential Englishness': the absolute ratification of a limited and specializing consensual process. To oppose the terms of this ratification was to be 'against literature'.

It is one of the signs of the success of this categorization of literature that even Marxism has made so little headway against it. Marx himself, to be sure, hardly tried. His characteristically intelligent and informed incidental discussions of actual literature are now often cited, defensively, as evidence of the humane flexibility of Marxism, when they ought really to be cited (with no particular devaluation) as evidence of how far he remained, in these matters, within the conventions and categories of his time. The radical challenge of the emphasis on 'practical consciousness' was thus never carried through to the categories of 'literature' and 'the aesthetic', and there was always hesitation about the practical application, in this area, of propositions which were held to be central and decisive almost everywhere else.

When such application was eventually made, in the later Marxist tradition, it was of three main kinds: an attempted assimilation of 'literature' to 'ideology', which was in practice little more than banging one inadequate category against another; an effective and important inclusion of 'popular literature'—the 'literature of the people'—as a necessary but neglected part of the 'literary tradition'; and a sustained but uneven attempt to relate 'literature' to the social and economic history within which 'it' had been produced. Each of these last two attempts has been significant. In the former a 'tradition' has been genuinely extended. In the latter there has been an effective reconstitution, over wide areas, of historical social practice, which makes the abstraction of 'literary values' much more problematical, and which, more positively, allows new kinds of reading and new kinds of questions about 'the works themselves'. This has been known, especially, as 'Marxist criticism' (a radical variant of the established bourgeois practice) though other work has been done on quite different bases, from a wider social history and from wider conceptions of 'the people', 'the language', and 'the nation'.

It is significant that 'Marxist criticism' and 'Marxist literary studies' have been most successful, in ordinary terms, when they have worked within the received category of 'literature', which they may have extended or even revalued, but never radically questioned or opposed. By contrast, what looked like fundamental theoretical revaluation, in the attempted assimilation to 'ideology', was a disastrous failure, and fundamentally compromised, in this whole area, the status of Marxism itself. Yet for half a century now there have been other and more significant tendencies. Lukács contributed a profound revaluation of 'the aesthetic'. The Frankfurt School, with its special emphasis on art, undertook a sustained re-examination of 'artistic production', centred on the concept of 'mediation'. Goldmann undertook a radical revaluation of the 'creative subject'. Marxist variants of formalism undertook radical redefinition of the processes of writing, with new uses of the concepts of 'signs' and 'texts', and with a significantly related refusal of 'literature' as a category. The methods and problems indicated by these tendencies will be examined in detail later in this book.

Yet the crucial theoretical break is the recognition of 'literature' as a specializing social and historical category. It should be clear that this does not diminish its importance. Just because it is historical, a key concept of a major phase of a culture, it is decisive evidence of a particular form of the social development of language. Within its terms, work of outstanding and permanent importance was done, in specific social and cultural relationships. But what has been happening, in our own century, is a profound transformation of these relationships, directly connected with changes in the basic means of production. These changes are most evident in the new technologies of language, which have moved practice beyond the relatively uniform and specializing technology of print. The principal changes are the

electronic transmission and recording of speech and of writing
for speech, and the chemical and electronic composition and
transmission of images, in complex relations with speech and
with writing for speech, and including images which can themselves be 'written'. None of these means cancels print, or even
diminishes its specific importance, but they are not simple additions to it, or mere alternatives. In their complex connections
and interrelations they compose a new substantial practice in
social language itself, over a range from public address and
manifest representation to 'inner speech' and verbal thought.
For they are always more than new technologies, in the limited
sense. They are means of production, developed in direct if
complex relations with profoundly changing and extending
social and cultural relationships: changes elsewhere recognizable as deep political and economic transformations. It is in no
way surprising that the specialized concept of 'literature',
developed in precise forms of correspondence with a particular
social class, a particular organization of learning, and the
appropriate particular technology of print, should now be so
often invoked in retrospective, nostalgic, or reactionary moods,
as a form of opposition to what is correctly seen as a new phase of
civilization. The situation is historically comparable to that
invocation of the divine and the sacred, and of divine and sacred
learning, against the new humanist concept of literature, in the
difficult and contested transition from feudal to bourgeois
society.

What can then be seen as happening, in each transition, is a
historical development of social language itself: finding new
means, new forms and then new definitions of a changing practical consciousness. Many of the active values of 'literature' have
then to be seen, not as tied to the concept, which came to limit as
well as to summarize them, but as elements of a continuing and
changing practice which already substantially, and now at the
level of theoretical redefinition, is moving beyond its old forms.

4. Ideology

The concept of 'ideology' did not originate in Marxism and is still in no way confined to it. Yet it is evidently an important concept in almost all Marxist thinking about culture, and especially about literature and ideas. The difficulty then is that we have to distinguish three common versions of the concept, which are all common in Marxist writing. These are, broadly:

(i) a system of beliefs characteristic of a particular class or group;

(ii) a system of illusory beliefs—false ideas or false consciousness—which can be contrasted with true or scientific knowledge;

(iii) the general process of the production of meanings and ideas.

In one variant of Marxism, senses (i) and (ii) can be effectively combined. In a class society, all beliefs are founded on class position, and the systems of belief of all classes—or, quite commonly, of all classes preceding, and other than, the proletariat, whose formation is the project of the abolition of class society—are then in part or wholly false (illusory). The specific problems in this powerful general proposition have led to intense controversy within Marxist thought. It is not unusual to find some form of the proposition alongside uses of the simple sense (i), as in the characterization, for example by Lenin, of 'socialist ideology'. Another way of broadly retaining but distinguishing senses (i) and (ii) is to use sense (i) for systems of belief founded on class position, including that of the proletariat within class society, and sense (ii) for contrast with (in a broad sense) *scientific* knowledge of all kinds, which is based on reality rather than illusions. Sense (iii) undercuts most of these associations and distinctions, for the ideological process—the production of meanings and ideas—is then seen as general and universal, and ideology is either this process itself or the area of its study. Positions associated with senses (i) and (ii) are then brought to bear in Marxist ideological studies.

In this situation there can be no question of establishing,

except in polemics, a single 'correct' Marxist definition of ideology. It is more to the point to return the term and its variations to the issues within which it and these were formed; and specifically, first, to the historical development. We can then return to the issues as they now present themselves, and to the important controversies which the term and its variations reveal and conceal.

'Ideology' was coined as a term in the late eighteenth century, by the French philosopher Destutt de Tracy. It was intended to be a philosophical term for the 'science of ideas'. Its use depended on a particular understanding of the nature of 'ideas', which was broadly that of Locke and the empiricist tradition. Thus ideas were not to be and could not be understood in any of the older 'metaphysical' or 'idealist' senses. The science of ideas must be a natural science, since all ideas originate in man's experience of the world. Specifically, in Destutt, ideology is part of zoology:

We have only an incomplete knowledge of an animal if we do not know his intellectual faculties. Ideology is a part of Zoology, and it is especially in man that this part is important and deserves to be more deeply understood. (*Éléments d'idéologie*, 1801, Preface)

The description is characteristic of scientific empiricism. The 'real elements' of ideology are 'our intellectual faculties, their principal phenomena and their most evident circumstances'. The critical aspect of this emphasis was at once realized by one kind of opponent, the reactionary de Bonald: 'Ideology has replaced metaphysics . . . because modern philosophy sees no other ideas in the world but those of men'. De Bonald correctly related the scientific sense of ideology to the empiricist tradition which had passed from Locke through Condillac, pointing out its preoccupation with 'signs and their influence on thought' and summarizing its 'sad system' as a reduction of 'our thoughts' to 'transformed sensations'. 'All the characteristics of intelligence', de Bonald added, 'disappeared under the scalpel of this ideological dissection.'

The initial bearings of the concept of ideology are then very complex. It was indeed an assertion against metaphysics that there are 'no ideas in the world but those of men'. At the same time, intended as a branch of empirical science, 'ideology' was limited, by its philosophical assumptions, to a version of ideas as 'transformed sensations' and to a version of language as a 'system of signs' (based, as in Condillac, on an ultimately mathematical model). These limitations, with their characteristic abstraction of 'man' and 'the world', and with their reliance on the passive 'reception' and 'systematic association' of 'sensations', were not only 'scientific' and 'empirical' but were elements of a basically bourgeois view of human existence. The rejection of metaphysics was a characteristic gain, confirmed by the development of precise and systematic empirical enquiry. At the same time the effective exclusion of any social dimension —both the practical exclusion of social relationships implied in the model of 'man' and 'the world', and the characteristic displacement of necessary social relationships to a formal system, whether the 'laws of psychology' or language as a 'system of signs'—was a deep and apparently irrecoverable loss and distortion.

It is significant that the initial objection to the exclusion of any active conception of intelligence was made from generally reactionary positions, which sought to retain the sense of activity in its old metaphysical forms. It is even more significant, in the next stage of the development, that a derogatory sense of 'ideology' as 'impractical theory' or 'abstract illusion', first introduced from an evidently reactionary position by Napoleon, was taken over, though from a new position, by Marx.

Napoleon said:

It is to the doctrine of the ideologues—to this diffuse metaphysics, which in a contrived manner seeks to find the primary causes and on this foundation would erect the legislation of peoples, instead of adapting the laws to a knowledge of the human heart and of the lessons of history—to which one must attribute all the misfortunes which have befallen our beautiful France.*

Scott (*Napoleon*, 1827, vi. 251) summarized: 'Ideology, by which nickname the French ruler used to distinguish every species of theory, which, resting in no respect upon the basis of self-interest, could, he thought, prevail with none save hot-brained boys and crazed enthusiasts.'

Each element of this condemnation of 'ideology'—which became very well known and was often repeated in Europe and North America during the first half of the nineteenth century—was taken up and applied by Marx and Engels, in their

* Cited in A. Naess, *Democracy, Ideology, and Objectivity*, Oslo, 1956, 151.

early writings. It is the substantial content of their attack on their
German contemporaries in *The German Ideology* (1846). To find
'primary causes' in 'ideas' was seen as the basic error. There is
even the same tone of contemptuous practicality in the anecdote
in Marx's Preface:

Once upon a time an honest fellow had the idea that men were drowned
in water only because they were possessed with the idea of gravity. If
they were to knock this idea out of their heads, say by stating it to be a
superstition, a religious idea, they would be sublimely proof against
any danger from water. (*GI*, 2)

Abstract theories, separated from the 'basis of self-interest', were
then beside the point.

Of course the argument could not be left at this stage. In place
of Napoleon's conservative (and suitably vague) standard of
'knowledge of the human heart and of the lessons of history',
Marx and Engels introduced 'the real ground of history'—the
process of production and self-production—from which the
'origins and growth' of 'different theoretical products' could be
traced. The simple cynicism of the appeal to 'self-interest'
became a critical diagnosis of the real basis of all ideas:

the ruling ideas are nothing more than the ideal expression of the
dominant material relationships, the dominant material relationships
grasped as ideas. (*GI*, 39)

Yet already at this stage there were obvious complications.
'Ideology' became a polemical nickname for kinds of thinking
which neglected or ignored the material social process of which
'consciousness' was always a part:

Consciousness can never be anything else than conscious existence,
and the existence of men is their actual life-process. If in all ideology
men and their circumstances appear upside down as in a *camera
obscura*, this phenomenon arises just as much from their historical
life-process as the inversion of objects on the retina does from their
physical life-process. (*GI*, 14)

The emphasis is clear but the analogy is difficult. The physical
processes of the retina cannot reasonably be separated from the
physical processes of the brain, which, *as a necessarily connected activity*, control and 'rectify' the inversion. The *camera
obscura* was a conscious device for discerning proportions; the
inversion had in fact been corrected by adding another lens. In
one sense the analogies are no more than incidental, but they

probably relate to (though in fact, as examples, they work against) an underlying criterion of 'direct positive knowledge'. They are in a way very like the use of 'the idea of gravity' to refute the notion of the controlling power of ideas. If the idea had been not a practical and scientific understanding of a natural force but, say, an idea of 'racial superiority' or of 'the inferior wisdom of women', the argument might in the end have come out the same way but it would have had to pass through many more significant stages and difficulties.

This is also true even of the more positive definition:

We do not set out from what men say, imagine, conceive, nor from men as narrated, thought of, imagined, conceived, in order to arrive at men in the flesh. We set out from real, active men, and on the basis of their real life-process we demonstrate the development of the ideological reflexes and echoes of this life-process. The phantoms formed in the human brain are also, necessarily, sublimates of their material life-process, which is empirically verifiable and bound to material premisses. Morality, religion, metaphysics, all the rest of ideology and their corresponding forms of consciousness, thus no longer retain the semblance of independence. (GI, 14)

That 'ideology' should be deprived of its 'semblance of independence' is entirely reasonable. But the language of 'reflexes,' 'echoes', 'phantoms', and 'sublimates' is simplistic, and has in repetition been disastrous. It belongs to the naïve dualism of 'mechanical materialism', in which the idealist separation of 'ideas' and 'material reality' had been repeated, but with its priorities reversed. The emphasis on consciousness as inseparable from conscious existence, and then on conscious existence as inseparable from material social processes, is in effect lost in the use of this deliberately degrading vocabulary. The damage can be realized if we compare it for a moment with Marx's description of 'human labour' in Capital (i. 185-6):

We presuppose labour in a form that stamps it as exclusively human . . . What distinguishes the worst architect from the best of bees is this, that the architect raises his structure in imagination before he erects it in reality. At the end of every labour-process, we get a result that already existed in the imagination of the labourer at its commencement.

This goes perhaps even too much the other way, but its difference from the world of 'reflexes', 'echoes', 'phantoms', and 'sublimates' hardly needs to be stressed. Consciousness is seen from the beginning as part of the human material social process, and its products in 'ideas' are then as much part of this process as material products themselves. This, centrally, was the thrust of Marx's whole argument, but the point was lost, in this crucial area, by a temporary surrender to the cynicism of 'practical men' and, even more, to the abstract empiricism of a version of 'natural science'.

What had really been introduced, as a corrective to abstract empiricism, was the sense of material and social history as the real relationship between 'man' and 'nature'. But it is then very curious of Marx and Engels to abstract, in turn, the persuasive 'men in the flesh', at whom we 'arrive'. To begin by presupposing them, as the necessary starting-point, is right while we remember that they are therefore also conscious men. The decision not to set out from 'what men say, imagine, conceive, nor from men as narrated, thought of, imagined, conceived' is then at best a corrective reminder that there is other and sometimes harder evidence of what they have done. But it is also at its worst an objectivist fantasy: that the whole 'real life-process' can be known independently of language ('what men say') and of its records ('men as narrated'). For the very notion of history would become absurd if we did not look at 'men as narrated' (when, having died, they are hardly likely to be accessible 'in the flesh', and on which, inevitably, Marx and Engels extensively and repeatedly relied) as well as at that 'history of industry . . . as it objectively exists . . . an *open book of the human faculties* . . . a human *psychology* which can be directly apprehended' (EPM, 121), which they had decisively introduced against the exclusions of other historians. What they were centrally arguing was a new way of seeing the total relationships between this 'open book' and 'what men say' and 'men as narrated'. In a polemical response to the abstract history of ideas or of consciousness they made their main point but in one decisive area lost it again. This confusion is the source of the naïve reduction, in much subsequent Marxist thinking, of consciousness, imagination, art, and ideas to 'reflexes', 'echoes', 'phantoms', and 'sublimates', and then of a profound confusion in the concept of 'ideology'.

We can trace further elements of this failure if we examine those definitions of ideology which gain most of their force by contrast with what is not ideology. The most common of these contrasts is with what is called 'science'. For example:

Where speculation ends—in real life—there real, positive science begins: the representation of the practical activity, of the practical process of development of men. Empty talk about consciousness ceases, and real knowledge has to take its place. When reality is depicted, philosophy as an independent branch of activity loses its medium of existence. (GI, 17)

There are several difficulties here. The uses of 'consciousness' and 'philosophy' depend almost entirely on the main argument about the futility of separating consciousness and thought from the material social process. It is the separation that makes such consciousness and thought into ideology. But it is easy to see how the point could be taken, and has often been taken, in a quite different way. In a new kind of abstraction, 'consciousness' and 'philosophy' are separated, in their turn, from 'real knowledge' and from the 'practical process'. This is especially easy to do with the available language of 'reflexes', 'echoes', 'phantoms', and 'sublimates'. The result of this separation, against the original conception of an *indissoluble* process, is the farcical exclusion of consciousness from the 'development of men' and from 'real knowledge' of this development. But the former, at least, is impossible by any standard. All that can then be done to mask its absurdity is elaboration of the familiar two-stage model (the mechanical materialist reversal of the idealist dualism), in which there is *first* material social life and *then*, at some temporal or spatial distance, consciousness and 'its' products. This leads directly to simple reductionism: 'consciousness' and 'its' products can be *nothing but* 'reflections' of what has already occurred in the material social process.

It can of course be said from experience (that experience which produced the later anxious warnings and qualifications) that this is a poor practical way of trying to understand 'consciousness and its products': that these continually escape so simple a reductive equation. But this is a marginal point. The real point is that the separation and abstraction of 'consciousness and its products' as a 'reflective' or 'second-stage' process results in an ironic idealization of 'consciousness and its products' at this secondary level.

For 'consciousness and its products' are always, though in variable forms, parts of the material social process itself: whether as what Marx called the necessary element of 'imagination' in the labour process; or as the necessary conditions of associated labour, in language and in practical ideas of relationship; or, which is so often and significantly forgotten, in the real processes—all of them physical and material, most of them manifestly so—which are masked and idealized as 'consciousness and its products' but which, when seen without illusions, are themselves necessarily social material activities. What is in fact idealized, in the ordinary reductive view, is 'thinking' or 'imagining', and the only materialization of these abstracted processes is by a general reference back to the whole (and because abstracted then in effect complete) material social process. And what this version of Marxism especially overlooks is that 'thinking' and 'imagining' are from the beginning social processes (of course including that capacity for 'internalization' which is a necessary part of any social process between actual individuals) and that they become accessible only in unarguably physical and material ways: in voices, in sounds made by instruments, in penned or printed writing, in arranged pigments on canvas or plaster, in worked marble or stone. To exclude these material social processes from the material social process is the same error as to reduce all material social processes to mere technical means for some other abstracted 'life'. The 'practical process' of the 'development of men' necessarily includes them from the beginning, and as more than the technical means for some quite separate 'thinking' and 'imagining'.

What can then be said to be 'ideology', in its received negative form? It can of course be said that these processes, or some of them, come in variable forms (which is as undeniable as the variable forms of *any* production), and that some of these forms are 'ideology' while others are not. This is a tempting path, but it is usually not followed far, because there is a fool's beacon erected just a little way along it. This is the difficult concept of 'science'. We have to notice first a problem of translation. The German *Wissenschaft*, like the French *science*, has a much broader meaning than English *science* has had since the early nineteenth century. The broader meaning is in the area of 'systematic knowledge' or 'organized learning'. In English this has been largely specialized to such knowledge based on observation of the 'real world' (at first, and still persistently, within the categories of 'man' and 'the world') and on the significant distinction (and even opposition) between the formerly interchangeable words *experience* and *experiment*, the latter attracting, in the course of development, new senses of *empirical* and *positive*. It is then very difficult for any English reader to take the translated phrase of Marx and Engels—'real, positive science'—in anything other than this specialized sense. But two qualifications have then at once to be made. First, that the Marxist definition of the 'real world', by moving beyond the separated categories of 'man' and 'the world' and including, as central, the active material social process, had made any such simple transfer impossible:

If industry is conceived as an *exoteric* form of the realization of the *essential human faculties*, one is able to grasp also the human essence of Nature or the *natural* essence of man. The natural sciences will then abandon their abstract materialist, or rather, idealist, orientation, and will become the basis of a *human science* . . . One basis for life and another for *science* is *a priori* a falsehood. (EPM, 122)

This is an argument precisely against the categories of the English specialization of 'science'. But then, second, the actual progress of scientific rationality, especially in its rejection of metaphysics and in its triumphant escape from a limitation to observation, experiment, and inquiry within received religious and philosophical systems, was immensely attractive as a model for understanding society. Though the object of inquiry had been radically changed—from 'man' and 'the world' to an active, interactive, and in a key sense self-creating material social process—it was supposed, or rather hoped, that the methods, or at least the mood, could be carried over.

This sense of getting free of the ordinary assumptions of social inquiry, which usually began where it should have ended, with the forms and categories of a particular historical phase of society, is immensely important and was radically demonstrated in most of Marx's work. But it is very different from the uncritical use of 'science' and 'scientific', with deliberate references to and analogies from 'natural science', to describe the essentially *critical and historical* work which was actually undertaken. Engels, it is true, used these references and analogies much more often than Marx. 'Scientific socialism' became, under his influence, a polemical catchword. In practice it depends almost equally on a (justifiable) sense of systematic knowledge of society, based on observation and analysis of its processes of development (as distinct, say, from 'utopian' socialism, which projected a desirable future without close consideration of the past and present processes within which it had to be attained); and on a (false) association with the 'fundamental' or 'universal' 'laws' of natural science, which, even when they turned out to be 'laws' rather than effective working generalizations or hypotheses, were of a different kind because their objects of study were radically different.

The notion of 'science' has had a crucial effect, negatively, on the concept of 'ideology'. If 'ideology' is contrasted with 'real, positive science', in the sense of detailed and connected knowledge of 'the practical process of development of men', then the distinction may have significance as an indication of the received assumptions, concepts, and points of view which can be shown to prevent or distort such detailed and connected knowledge. We can often feel that this is all that was really intended. But the contrast is of course less simple than it may look, since its confident application depends on a knowable distinction between 'detailed and connected knowledge of the practical process of development' and other kinds of 'knowledge' which may often closely resemble it. One way of applying the distinguishing criterion would be by examining the 'assumptions, concepts, and points of view', whether received or not, by which any knowledge has been gained and organized. But it is just this kind of analysis which is prevented by the *a priori* assumption of a 'positive' method which is not subject to such scrutiny: an assumption based in fact on the received (and unexamined) assumptions of 'positive, scientific knowledge', freed of the 'ideological bias' of all other observers. This position, which has been often repeated in orthodox Marxism, is either a circular demonstration or a familiar partisan claim (of the kind made by almost all parties) that others are biased but that, by definition, we are not.

That indeed was the fool's way out of the very difficult problem which was now being confronted, within historical materialism. Its symptomatic importance at the level of dogma has to be noted and then set aside if we are to see, clearly, a very different and much more interesting proposition, which leads to a quite different (though not often theoretically distinguished) definition of ideology. This begins from the main point of the attack on the Young Hegelians, who were said to "consider conceptions, thoughts, ideas, in fact all the products of consciousness, to which they attribute an independent existence, as the real chains of men". Social liberation would then come through a 'change of consciousness'. Everything then turns, of course, on the definition of 'consciousness'. The definition adopted, polemically, by Marx and Engels, is in effect their definition of ideology: not 'practical consciousness' but 'self-dependent theory'. Hence 'really it is only a question of explaining this theoretical talk from the actual existing conditions. The real, practical dissolution of these phrases, the removal of these notions from the consciousness of men, will. . . . be effected by altered circumstances, not by theoretical deductions' (*GI*, 15). In this task the proletariat has an advantage, since 'for the mass of men . . . these theoretical notions do not exist'.

If we can take this seriously we are left with a much more limited and in that respect more plausible definition of ideology. Since 'consciousness', including 'conceptions, thoughts, ideas', can hardly be asserted to be non-existent in the 'mass of men', the definition falls back to a *kind* of consciousness, and certain *kinds* of conceptions, thoughts, and ideas, which are specifically 'ideological'. Engels later sought to clarify this position:

Every ideology . . . once it has arisen, develops in connection with the given concept-material, and develops this material further; otherwise it would cease to be ideology, that is, occupation with thoughts as with independent entities, developing independently and subject only to their own laws. That the material life conditions of the persons inside whose heads this thought process goes on, in the last resort determines the course of this process, remains of necessity unknown to these persons, for otherwise there would be an end to all ideology. (*Feuerbach*, 65-6)

Ideology is a process accomplished by the so-called thinker, consciously indeed but with a false consciousness. The real motives impelling him remain unknown to him, otherwise it would not be an ideological process at all. Hence he imagines false or apparent motives. Because it is a process of thought he derives both its form and its content from pure thought, either his own or that of his predecessors.*

Taken on their own, these statements can appear virtually psychological. They are structurally very similar to the Freudian concept of 'rationalization' in such phrases as 'inside whose heads'; 'real motives . . . unknown to him'; 'imagines false or

---

* Letter to F. Mehring, 14 July 1893 (*Marx and Engels: Selected Correspondence*, New York, 1935).

apparent motives'. In this form a version of 'ideology' is readily accepted in modern bourgeois thought, which has its own concepts of the 'real'—material or psychological—to undercut either ideology or rationalization. But it had once been a more serious position. Ideology was specifically identified as a consequence of the division of labour:

> Division of labour only becomes truly such from the moment when a division of material and mental labour appears . . . From this moment onwards consciousness *can* really flatter itself that it is something other than consciousness of existing practice, that it *really* represents something without representing something real; from now on consciousness is in a position to emancipate itself from the world and to proceed to the formation of 'pure' theory, theology, philosophy, ethics, etc. (*GI*, 51)

Ideology is then 'separated theory', and its analysis must involve restoration of its 'real' connections.

> The division of labour . . . manifests itself also in the ruling class as the division of mental and material labour, so that inside this class one part appears as the thinkers of the class (its active, conceptive ideologists, who make the perfecting of the illusion of the class about itself their chief source of livelihood) while the other's attitude to these ideas and illusions is more passive and receptive, because they are in reality the active members of this class and have less time to make up illusions and ideas about themselves. (*GI*, 39-40)

This is shrewd enough, as is the later observation that

> each new class . . . is compelled . . . to represent its interest as the common interest of all the members of society, put in an ideal form; it will give its ideas the form of universality, and represent them as the only rational, universally valid ones. (*GI*, 40-1)

But 'ideology' then hovers between 'a system of beliefs characteristic of a certain class' and 'a system of illusory beliefs—false ideas or false consciousness—which can be contrasted with true or scientific knowledge'.

This uncertainty was never really resolved. Ideology as 'separated theory'—the natural home of illusions and false consciousness—is itself separated from the (intrinsically limited) 'practical consciousness of a class'. This separation, however, is very much easier to carry out in theory than in practice. The immense body of direct class-consciousness, directly expressed and again and again directly imposed, can appear to escape the taint of 'ideology', which would be limited to the 'universalizing' philosophers. But then what name is to be found for these powerful direct systems? Surely not 'true' or 'scientific' knowledge, except by an extraordinary sleight-of-hand with the description 'practical'. For most ruling classes have not needed to be 'unmasked'; they have usually proclaimed their existence and the 'conceptions, thoughts, ideas' which ratify it. To overthrow them is ordinarily to overthrow their conscious practice, and this is always very much harder than overthrowing their 'abstract' and 'universalizing' ideas, which also, in real terms, have a much more complicated and interactive relationship with the dominant 'practical consciousness' than any merely dependent or illusory concepts could ever have. Or again, 'the existence of revolutionary ideas in a particular period presupposes the existence of a revolutionary class'. But this may or may not be true, since all the difficult questions are about the development of a pre-revolutionary or potentially revolutionary or briefly revolutionary into a sustained revolutionary class, and the same difficult questions necessarily arise about pre-revolutionary, potentially revolutionary, or briefly revolutionary ideas. Marx and Engels's own complicated relations to the (in itself very complicated) revolutionary character of the European proletariat is an intensely practical example of just this difficulty, as is also their complicated and acknowledged relationship (including the relationship implied by critique) to their intellectual predecessors.

What really happened, in temporary but influential substitution for just this detailed and connected knowledge, was, first, an abstraction of 'ideology', as a category of illusions and false consciousness (an abstraction which as they had best reason to know would prevent examination, not of the abstracted ideas, which is relatively easy, but of the material social process in which 'conceptions, thoughts, ideas', of course in different degrees, become practical). Second, in relation to this, the abstraction was given a categorical rigidity, an *epochal* rather than a genuinely historical consciousness of ideas, which could then be mechanically separated into forms of successive and unified stages of—but which? – both knowledge and illusion. Each stage of the abstraction is radically different, in both theory and practice, from Marx's emphasis on a necessary conflict of real interests, in the material social process, and on the "legal, political, religious, aesthetic, or philosophical—in short

ideological—forms in which men become conscious of this conflict and fight it out". The infection from categorical argument
against specialists in categories has here been burned out, by a
practical recognition of the whole and indissoluble material and
social process. 'Ideology' then reverts to a specific and practical
dimension: the complicated process within which men
'become' (are) conscious of their interests and their conflicts.
The categorical short-cut to an (abstract) distinction between
'true' and 'false' consciousness is then effectively abandoned, as
in all practice it has to be.

All these varying uses of 'ideology' have persisted within the
general development of Marxism. There has been a convenient
dogmatic retention, at some levels, of ideology as 'false consciousness'. This has often prevented the more specific analysis
of operative distinctions of 'true' and 'false' consciousness at the
practical level, which is always that of social relationships, and
of the part played in these relationships by 'conceptions,
thoughts, ideas'. There was a late attempt, by Lukács, to clarify
this analysis by a distinction between 'actual consciousness'
and 'imputed' or 'potential' consciousness (a full and 'true'
understanding of a real social position). This has the merit of
avoiding the reduction of all 'actual consciousness' to ideology,
but the category is speculative, and indeed *as a category* cannot
easily be sustained. In *History and Class-Consciousness* it
depended on a last abstract attempt to identify truth with the
idea of the proletariat, but in this Hegelian form it is no more
convincing than the earlier positivist identification of a category
of 'scientific knowledge'. A more interesting but equally difficult attempt to define 'true' consciousness was the elaboration
of Marx's point about changing the world rather than interpreting it. What became known as the 'test of practice' was offered as
a criterion of truth and as the essential distinction from ideology. In certain general ways this is a wholly consistent projection from the idea of 'practical consciousness', but it is easy to
see how its application to specific theories, formulations, and
programmes can result either in a vulgar 'success' ethic, mas-
querading as 'historical truth', or in numbness or confusion
when there are practical defeats and deformations. The 'test of
practice', that is to say, cannot be applied to 'scientific theory'
and 'ideology' taken as abstract categories. The real point of the
definition of 'practical consciousness' was indeed to undercut

these abstractions, which nevertheless have continued to be reproduced as 'Marxist theory'.

Three other tendencies in twentieth-century concepts of ideology may be briefly noted. First, the concept has been commonly used, within Marxism and outside it, in the relatively neutral sense of 'a system of beliefs characteristic of a particular class or group' (without implications of 'truth' or 'illusion' but with positive reference to a social situation and interest and its defining or constitutive system of meanings and values). It is thus possible to speak neutrally or even approvingly of 'socialist ideology'. A curious example here is that of Lenin:

> Socialism, in so far as it is the ideology of struggle of the proletarian class, undergoes the general conditions of birth, development and consolidation of any ideology, that is to say it is founded on all the material of human knowledge, it presupposes a high level of science, scientific work, etc. . . . . In the class struggle of the proletariat which develops spontaneously, as an elemental force, on the basis of capitalist relations, socialism is *introduced* by the ideologists.*

Obviously 'ideology' here is not intended as 'false consciousness'. The distinction between a class and its ideologists can be related to the distinction made by Marx and Engels, but one crucial clause of this—'active, conceptive ideologists, who make the perfecting of the illusion of the class about itself their chief source of livelihood'—has then to be tacitly dropped, unless the reference to a 'ruling class' can be dressed up as a saving clause. More significantly, perhaps, 'ideology' in its now neutral or approving sense is seen as 'introduced' on the foundation of 'all . . . human knowledge, . . . science . . . etc', of course brought to bear from a class point of view. The position is clearly that ideology is theory and that theory is at once secondary and necessary; 'practical consciousness', as here of the proletariat, will not itself produce it. This is radically different from Marx's thinking, where all 'separate' theory is ideology, and where genuine theory—'real, positive knowledge'—is, by contrast, the articulation of 'practical consciousness'. But Lenin's model corresponds to one orthodox sociological formulation, in which there is 'social situation' and there is also 'ideology', their relations variable but certainly neither dependent nor 'determined', thus allowing both their separate and their comparative history

*'Letter to the Federation of the North', *Collected Works*, Moscow, 1961; 6, 163.

and analysis. Lenin's formulation also echoes, from a quite opposite political position, Napoleon's identification of 'the ideologists', who *bring ideas* to 'the people', for their liberation or destruction according to point of view. The Napoleonic definition, in an unaltered form, has of course also persisted, as a popular form of criticism of political struggles which are defined by ideas or even by principles. 'Ideology' (the product of 'doctrinaires') is then contrasted with 'practical experience', 'practical politics', and what is known as pragmatism. This general sense of 'ideology' as not only 'doctrinaire' and 'dogmatic' but as *a priori* and abstract has co-existed uneasily with the equally general (neutral or approving) descriptive sense.

Finally there is an obvious need for a general term to describe not only the products but the processes of all signification, including the signification of values. It is interesting that 'ideology' and 'ideological' have been widely used in this sense. Vološinov, for example, uses 'ideological' to describe the process of the production of meaning through signs, and 'ideology' is taken as the dimension of social experience in which meanings and values are produced. The difficult relation of so wide a sense to the other senses which we have seen to be active hardly needs stressing. Yet, however far the term itself may be compromised, some form of this emphasis on signification as a central social process is necessary. In Marx, in Engels, and in much of the Marxist tradition the central argument about 'practical consciousness' was limited and frequently distorted by failures to see that the fundamental processes of social signification are intrinsic to 'practical consciousness' and intrinsic also to the 'conceptions, thoughts, and ideas' which are *recognizable* as its products. The limiting condition within 'ideology' as a concept, from its beginning in Destutt, was the tendency to limit processes of meaning and valuation to formed, separable 'ideas' or 'theories'. To attempt to take these back to 'a world of sensations' or, on the other hand, to a 'practical consciousness' or a 'material social process' which has been so defined as to exclude these fundamental signifying processes, or to make them essentially secondary, is the persistent thread of error. For the practical links between 'ideas' and 'theories' and the 'production of real life' are all in this material social process of signification itself.

Moreover, when this is realized, those 'products' which are

not ideas or theories, but which are the very different works we call 'art' and 'literature', and which are normal elements of the very general processes we call 'culture' and 'language', can be approached in ways other than reduction, abstraction, or assimilation. This is the argument that has now to be taken into cultural and literary studies, and especially into the Marxist contribution to them, which, in spite of appearances, is then likely to be even more controversial than hitherto. But it is then an open question whether 'ideology' and 'ideological', with their senses of 'abstraction' and 'illusion', or their senses of 'ideas' and 'theories', or even their senses of a 'system' of beliefs or of meanings and values, are sufficiently precise and practicable terms for so far-reaching and radical a redefinition.

II. Cultural Theory

1. Base and Superstructure

Any modern approach to a Marxist theory of culture must begin by considering the proposition of a determining base and a determined superstructure. From a strictly theoretical point of view this is not, in fact, where we might choose to begin. It would be in many ways preferable if we could begin from a proposition which originally was equally central, equally authentic: namely the proposition that social being determines consciousness. It is not that the two propositions necessarily deny each other or are in contradiction. But the proposition of base and superstructure, with its figurative element and with its suggestion of a fixed and definite spatial relationship, constitutes, at least in certain hands, a very specialized and at times unacceptable version of the other proposition. Yet in the transition from Marx to Marxism, and in the development of mainstream Marxism itself, the proposition of the determining base and the determined superstructure has been commonly held to be the key to Marxist cultural analysis.

The source of this proposition is commonly taken to be a well-known passage in Marx's 1859 Preface to *A Contribution to the Critique of Political Economy*:

In the social production of their life, men enter into definite relations that are indispensable and independent of their will, relations of production which correspond to a definite stage of development of their material productive forces. The sum total of these relations of production constitutes the economic structure of society, the real foundation, on which rises a legal and political superstructure and to which correspond definite forms of social consciousness. The mode of production of material life conditions the social, political and intellectual life process in general. It is not the consciousness of men that determines their being, but, on the contrary, their social being that determines their consciousness. At a certain stage of their development, the material productive forces of society come in conflict with the existing relations of production or—what is but a legal expression for the same thing—with the property relations within which they have been at work hitherto. From forms of development of the productive forces these relations turn into their fetters. Then begins an epoch of social revolution. With the change of the economic foundation the entire immense superstructure is more or less rapidly transformed. In considering such transformations a distinction should always be made between the material transformation of the economic conditions of production, which can be determined with the precision of natural science, and the legal, political, religious, aesthetic or philosophic—in short, ideological—forms in which men become conscious of this conflict and fight it out. (SW 1. 362-4)

This is hardly an obvious starting-point for any cultural theory. It is part of an exposition of historical materialist method in the understanding of legal relations and forms of state. The first use of the term 'superstructure' is explicitly qualified as 'legal and political'. (It should incidentally be noted that the English translation in most common use has a plural—"legal and political superstructures"—for Marx's singular "juristicher und politischer Überbau".) 'Definite forms of social consciousness' are further said to 'correspond' to it (entsprechen). Transformation of the 'entire immense superstructure', in the social revolution which begins from the altered relations of productive forces and relations of production, is a process in which 'men become conscious of this conflict and fight it out' in 'ideological forms' which now include the 'religious, aesthetic, or philosophic' as well as the legal and political. Much has been deduced from this formulation, but the real context is inevitably limited. Thus it would be possible, simply from this passage, to define 'cultural' ('religious, aesthetic or philosophic') forms in which 'men become conscious of this conflict', without necessarily supposing that these specific forms are the whole of 'cultural' activity.

There is at least one earlier use, by Marx, of the term 'superstructure'. It is in *The Eighteenth Brumaire of Louis Napoleon*, 1851-2:

Upon the several forms of property, upon the social conditions of existence, a whole superstructure is reared of various and peculiarly shaped feelings (empfindungen), illusions, habits of thought and conceptions of life. The whole class produces and shapes these out of its material foundation and out of the corresponding social conditions. The individual unit to whom they flow through tradition and education may fancy that they constitute the true reasons for and premises of his conduct. (SW 1. 272-3)

This is an evidently different use. The 'superstructure' is here the whole 'ideology' of the class: its 'form of consciousness'; its constitutive ways of seeing itself in the world. It would be possible, from this and the later use, to see three senses of 'superstructure' emerging: (a) legal and political forms which express existing real relations of production; (b) forms of consciousness which express a particular class view of the world; (c) a process in which, over a whole range of activities, men become conscious of a fundamental economic conflict and fight it out. These three senses would direct our attention, respectively, to (a) institutions; (b) forms of consciousness; (c) political and cultural practices.

It is clear that these three areas are related and must, in analysis, be interrelated. But on just this crucial question of interrelation the term itself is of little assistance, just because it is variably applied to each area in turn. Nor is this at all surprising, since the use is not primarily conceptual, in any precise way, but metaphorical. What it primarily expresses is the important sense of a visible and formal 'superstructure' which might be analysed on its own but which cannot be understood without seeing that it rests on a 'foundation'. The same point must be made of the corresponding metaphorical term. In the use of 1851-2 it is absent, and the origins of a particular form of class consciousness are specified as 'forms of property' and 'social conditions of existence'. In the use of 1859 it appears in almost conscious metaphor: 'the economic structure of society—the real foundation (*die reale Basis*), on which rises (*erhebt*) a legal and political superstructure (*Überbau*)'. It is replaced, later in the argument, by 'the economic foundation' (*ökonomische Grundlage*). The continuity of meaning is relatively clear, but the variation of terms for one part of the relationship ('forms of property, social conditions of existence'; 'economic structure of society'; 'real basis'; 'real foundation'; *Basis*; *Grundlage*) is not matched by explicit variation of the other term of the relationship, though the actual signification of this term (*Überbau*; superstructure) is, as we have seen, variable. It is part of the complexity of the subsequent argument that the term rendered in English explication (probably first by Engels) as 'base' is rendered in other languages in significant variations (in French usually as *infrastructure*, in Italian as *struttura*, and so on, with some complicating effects on the substance of the argument).

In the transition from Marx to Marxism, and then in the development of expository and didactic formulations, the words used in the original arguments were projected, first, as if they were precise concepts, and second, as if they were descriptive terms for observable 'areas' of social life. The main sense of the words in the original arguments had been relational, but the popularity of the terms tended to indicate either (a) relatively enclosed categories or (b) relatively enclosed areas of activity. These were then correlated either temporally (first material production, then consciousness, then politics and culture) or in effect, forcing the metaphor, spatially (visible and distinguishable 'levels' or 'layers'—politics and culture, then forms of consciousness, and so on down to 'the base'). The serious practical problems of method, which the original words had indicated, were then usually in effect bypassed by methods derived from a confidence, rooted in the popularity of the terms, in the relative enclosure of categories or areas expressed as 'the base', 'the superstructure'.

It is then ironic to remember that the force of Marx's original criticism had been mainly directed against the *separation* of 'areas' of thought and activity (as in the separation of consciousness from material production) and against the related evacuation of specific content—real human activities—by the imposition of abstract categories. The common abstraction of 'the base' and 'the superstructure' is thus a radical persistence of the modes of thought which he attacked. That in the course of other arguments he gave some warrant for this, within the intrinsic difficulties of any such formulation, is certainly true. But it is significant that when he came to any sustained analysis, or to a realization of the need for such analysis, he was at once specific and flexible in his use of his own terms. He had already observed, in the formulation of 1859, a distinction between analysing 'the economic conditions of production, which can be determined with the precision of natural science' and the analysis of 'ideological forms', for which methods were evidently less precise. In 1857 he had noted:

As regards art, it is well known that some of its peaks by no means correspond to the general development of society; nor do they therefore to the material substructure, the skeleton as it were of its organization.

His solution of the problem he then discusses, that of Greek art, is hardly convincing, but the 'by no means correspond' is a characteristic practical recognition of the complexity of real relations. Engels, in his essay *Feuerbach and the End of Classical German Philosophy*, still argued specifically, showing how the 'economic basis' of a political struggle could be dulled in consciousness or altogether lost sight of, and how a legal system could be projected as independent of its economic content, in the course of its professional development. Then:

> Still higher ideologies, that is, such as are still further removed from the material, economic basis, take the form of philosophy and religion. Hence the interconnection between conceptions and their material conditions of existence becomes more and more complicated, more and more obscured by intermediate links. But the interconnection exists.

This relational emphasis, including not only complexity but recognition of the ways in which some connections are lost to consciousness, is of course very far from the abstract categories (though it supports the implication of separate areas) of 'super-structure' and 'base'.

In all serious Marxist analysis the categories are of course not used abstractly. But they may have their effect none the less. It is significant that the first phase of the recognition of practical complexities stressed what are really *quantitative* relations. By the end of the nineteenth century it was common to recognize what can best be described as disturbances, or special difficulties, of an otherwise regular relationship. This is true of the idea of 'lags' in time, which had been developed from Marx's observation that some of the 'peaks' of art 'by no means correspond to the general development of society'. This could be expressed (though Marx's own 'solution' to this problem had not been of this kind) as a matter of *temporal* 'delay' or 'unevenness'. The same basic model is evident in Engels's notion of the relative *distance* ('still further removed') of the 'higher ideologies'. Or consider Engels's letter to Bloch of September 1890:

> According to the materialist conception of history, the *ultimately* determining element in history is the production and reproduction of real life. More than this neither Marx nor I have ever asserted. Hence if somebody twists this into saying that the economic element is the *only* determining one, he transforms that proposition into a meaningless, abstract, senseless phrase. The economic situation is the basis, but the various elements of the superstructure—political forms of the class struggle and its results, to wit: constitutions established by the victorious class after a successful battle, etc., juridical forms, and even the reflexes of all these actual struggles in the brains of the participants, political, juristic, philosophical theories, religious views and their further development into systems of dogma—also exercise their influence upon the course of the historical struggles and in many cases

preponderate in determining their *form*. There is an interaction of all these elements in which, amid all the endless host of accidents (that is, of things and events whose inner interconnection is so remote or so impossible of proof that we can regard it as non-existent, as negligible), the economic movement finally asserts itself as necessary. Otherwise the application of the theory to any period of history would be easier than the solution of a simple equation of the first degree.

This is a vital acknowledgement of real and methodological complexities. It is particularly relevant to the idea of 'determination', which will be separately discussed, and to the decisive problem of consciousness as 'reflexes' or 'reflection'. But within the vigour of his contrast between real history and a 'meaningless, abstract, senseless phrase', and alongside his recognition of a new (and theoretically significant) exception—'the endless host of accidents'—Engels does not so much revise the enclosed categories—'the basis' ('the economic element', 'the economic situation', 'the economic movement') and 'the various elements' (political, juridical, theoretical) of 'the superstructure'—as reiterate the categories and instance certain exceptions, indirectnesses, and irregularities which obscure their otherwise regular relation. What is fundamentally lacking, in the theoretical formulations of this important period, is any adequate recognition of the indissoluble connections between material production, political and cultural institutions and activity, and consciousness. The classic summary of 'the relationship between the base and the superstructure' is Plekhanov's distinction of 'five sequential elements: (i) the state of productive forces; (ii) the economic conditions; (iii) the socio-political regime; (iv) the psyche of social man; (v) various ideologies reflecting the properties of this psyche' (*Fundamental Problems of Marxism*, Moscow, 1922, 76). This is better than the bare projection of 'a base' and 'a superstructure', which has been so common. But what is wrong with it is its description of these 'elements' as 'sequential', when they are in practice indissoluble: not in the sense that they cannot be distinguished for purposes of analysis, but in the decisive sense that these are not separate 'areas' or 'elements' but the whole, specific activities and products of real men. That is to say, the analytic categories, as so often in idealist thought, have, almost unnoticed, become substantive descriptions, which then take habitual priority over the whole social process to which, as analytic categories, they are attempting to speak. Orthodox analysts began to think of 'the base' and 'the superstructure' as if they were separable concrete entities. In doing so they lost sight of the very processes—not abstract relations but constitutive processes—which it should have been the special function of historical materialism to emphasize. I shall be discussing later the major theoretical response to this loss: the attempt to reconstitute such processes by the idea of 'mediation'.

A persistent dissatisfaction, within Marxism, about the proposition of 'base and superstructure', has been most often expressed by an attempted refinement and revaluation of 'the superstructure'. Apologists have emphasized its complexity, substance, and 'autonomy' or autonomous value. Yet most of the difficulty still lies in the original extension of metaphorical terms for a relationship into abstract categories or concrete areas *between which* connections are looked for and complexities or relative autonomies emphasized. It is actually more important to observe the character of this extension in the case of 'the base' than in the case of the always more varied and variable 'superstructure'. By extension and by habit, 'the base' has come to be considered virtually as an object (a particular and reductive version of 'material existence'). Or, in specification, 'the base' is given very general and apparently uniform properties. 'The base' is the real social existence of man. 'The base' is the real relations of production corresponding to a stage of the development of material productive forces. 'The base' is a mode of production at a particular stage of its development. Of course these are, in practice, different propositions. Yet each is also very different from Marx's central emphasis on productive *activities*. He had himself made the point against reduction of 'the base' to a category:

In order to study the connexion between intellectual and material production it is above all essential to conceive the latter in its determined historical form and not as a general category. For example, there corresponds to the capitalist mode of production a type of intellectual production quite different from that which corresponded to the medieval mode of production. Unless material production itself is understood in its specific historical form, it is impossible to grasp the characteristics of the intellectual production which corresponds to it or the reciprocal action between the two. (*Theorien über den Mehrwert*, cit. Bottomore and Rubel, 96–7.)

We can add that while a particular stage of 'real social existence', or of 'relations of production', or of a 'mode of production', can be discovered and made precise by analysis, it is never, as a body of activities, either uniform or static. It is one of the central propositions of Marx's sense of history, for example, that in actual development there are deep contradictions in the relationships of production and in the consequent social relationships. There is therefore the continual possibility of the dynamic variation of these forces. The 'variations' of the superstructure might be deduced from this fact alone, were it not that the 'objective' implications of 'the base' reduce all such variations to secondary consequences. It is only when we realize that 'the base', to which it is habitual to *refer* variations, is itself a dynamic and internally contradictory process—the specific activities and modes of activity, over a range from association to antagonism, of real men and classes of men—that we can begin to free ourselves from the notion of an 'area' or a 'category' with certain fixed properties for deduction to the variable processes of a 'superstructure'. The physical fixity of the terms exerts a constant pressure against just this realization.

Thus, contrary to a development in Marxism, it is not 'the base' and 'the superstructure' that need to be studied, but specific and indissoluble real processes, within which the decisive relationship, from a Marxist point of view, is that expressed by the complex idea of 'determination'.

2. Determination

No problem in Marxist cultural theory is more difficult than that of 'determination'. According to its opponents, Marxism is a necessarily reductive and determinist kind of theory: no cultural activity is allowed to be real and significant in itself, but is always reduced to a direct or indirect expression of some preceding and controlling economic content, or of a political content determined by an economic position or situation. In the perspective of mid-twentieth century developments of Marxism, this description can be seen as a caricature. Certainly it is often asserted with a confidence as solid as it is out of date. Yet it can hardly be denied that it came, with all its difficulties, from a common form of Marxism. Of course within that form, and in more recent Marxist thinking, there have been many qualifications of the idea of determination, of the kind noted in Engels's letter to Bloch, or of an apparently more radical kind, such as the contemporary idea of 'overdetermination' (a difficult term in English, since its intended meaning is determination by multiple factors). Some of these revisions have in effect dropped the original Marxist emphasis, in attempted syntheses with other orders of determination in psychology (a revised Freudianism) or in mental or formal structures (formalism, structuralism). These qualifications and revisions certainly indicate the inherent difficulties of the proposition. But at the same time they are welcomed by those opponents of Marxism who want to evade its continued challenge or, more directly, dismiss it as irrelevant dogma. It is then crucial to be certain what that challenge was and is. A Marxism without some concept of determination is in effect worthless. A Marxism with many of the concepts of determination it now has is quite radically disabled.

We can begin with the apparent source of the proposition, in the well-known passage from the 1859 Preface. As we read this in Marx's German, especially alongside the English translations, we become aware, inevitably, of the linguistic complexities of the word 'determine'. Marx's normal word is *bestimmen*; it occurs four times in the passage quoted earlier in translation.

The English 'determine' occurs three times in the translation. One of these uses is a formal repetition not present in the original; another is a translation of a quite different word, *konstatieren*. The point here is not so much the adequacy of the translation as the extraordinary linguistic complexity of this group of words. This can best be illustrated by considering the complexity of 'determine' in English.

The root sense of 'determine' is 'setting bounds' or 'setting limits'. In its extraordinarily varied development, in application to many specific processes, it is the sense of putting a limit and therefore an end to some action that is most problematical. The determination of a calculation, a course of study, or a lease is, as an idea, relatively simple. Determination by an authority is at first simple, but is the source of most of the special difficulties, in its implication of something beyond and even external to the specific action which nevertheless decides or settles it. The sense of externality is decisive in the development of the concept of 'determinism', in which some power (God or Nature or History) controls or decides the outcome of an action or process, beyond or irrespective of the wills or desires of its agents. This is abstract determinism, to be distinguished from an often apparently similar inherent determinism, in which the essential character of a process or the properties of its components are held to determine (control) its outcome: the character and properties are then 'determinants'. What had been (abstractly) the 'determinat Counsell and foreknowledge of God' (Tyndale) became, especially in the physical sciences, 'determinate conditions' 'or 'determined laws', based on precise knowledge of the inherent characteristics of a process and its components. The abstract idea presupposes a powerlessness (or unsurpassable limits to the power) of the participants in an action. The 'scientific' idea presupposes unalterable or relatively fixed characteristics; change is then a matter of altered (but discoverable and in that sense predictable) conditions and combinations.

It seems clear that the Marxist version of determinism, at least in its first stage, corresponds to this 'scientific' idea.

In the social production which men carry on they enter into definite relations that are indispensable and independent of their will . . . a definite stage of development . . . (*SW*, i. 362)

The English 'definite' translates Marx's forms of *bestimmen*.

The existing stage of material production, and the social relations corresponding to it, are in that sense 'fixed'.

The mass of productive forces accessible to men determines the conditions of society . . . (*GI*, 18)

From this sense of determined conditions it is easy to understand the development of a Marxism which stressed the 'iron laws', the 'absolutely objective conditions', of an 'economy', from which all else followed. In this influential interpretation, Marxism had discovered the 'laws' of an objective external system of economy, and everything then followed, sooner or later, directly or indirectly, from these laws. But this is not the only way in which the sense can be developed. It is as reasonable, remembering 'enter into' and 'accessible to', to stress the predominance of objective conditions at any particular moment in the process. This turns out, in practice, to be a quite different claim. It is what Engels wrote, defensively, in his letter to Bloch: 'We make our history ourselves, but, in the first place, under very definite assumptions and conditions'. What this restores, as against the alternative development, is the idea of direct agency: 'we make our history ourselves'. The 'definite' or 'objective' assumptions and conditions are then the qualifying terms of this agency: in fact 'determination' as 'the setting of limits'.

The radical difference between 'determination' in this sense, and 'determination' in the sense of the 'laws' of a whole process, subject to inherent and predictable development, is not difficult to grasp but can often slip away in the shifting senses of 'determine'. The key question is the degree to which the 'objective' conditions are seen as *external*. Since, by definition, within Marxism, the objective conditions are and can only be the result of human actions in the material world, the real distinction can be only between *historical* objectivity—the conditions into which, at any particular point in time, men find themselves born, thus the 'accessible' conditions into which they 'enter'—and *abstract* objectivity, in which the 'determining' process is 'independent of their will' not in the historical sense that they have inherited it but in the absolute sense that they cannot control it; they can seek only to understand it and guide their actions accordingly.

This abstract objectivity is the basis of what became widely known, in Marxism, as 'economism'. As a philosophical and political doctrine it is worthless, but it has then in turn to be understood historically. The strongest single reason for the development of abstract determinism is the historical experience of large-scale capitalist economy, in which many more people than Marxists concluded that control of the process was beyond them, that it was at least in practice external to their wills and desires, and that it had therefore to be seen as governed by its own 'laws'. Thus, with bitter irony, a critical and revolutionary doctrine was changed, not only in practice but at this level of principle, into the very forms of passivity and reification against which an alternative sense of 'determination' had set out to operate.

Abstract determinism, that is to say, has to be seen as in one sense determined. It is a form of response and interpretation that is conditioned by its experience of real historical limits. The decisive difference between 'determinate' natural laws and 'determinate' social processes was overlooked—in part by a confusion of language, in part from specific historical experience. The description of both kinds of knowledge as 'scientific' compounded the confusion. But is it then possible to return to a sense of 'determination' as the experience of 'objective limits'? As a negative sense this is undoubtedly important, and Marx used it repeatedly. New social relations, and the new kinds of activity that are possible through them, may be imagined but cannot be achieved unless the determining limits of a particular mode of production are surpassed in practice, by actual social change. This was the history, for example, of the Romantic impulse to human liberation, in its actual interaction with a dominant capitalism.

But to say only this is to be in danger of falling back into a new passive and objectivist model. This is what happened to Engels:

The historical event . . . may . . . be viewed as the product of a power which works as a whole unconsciously and without volition. For what each individual wills is obstructed by everyone else, and what emerges is something that no one willed.*

Here society is the objectified (unconscious and unwilled) general process, and the only alternative forces are 'individual

* Letter to J. Bloch, 1890 (*Marx and Engels: Selected Correspondence*, New York, 1935, 476).

wills'. But this is a bourgeois version of society. A particular form of this version was later specified in Freudianism, and is the real ground for the Marxist–Freudian syntheses which, ironically, have been the main opposition to economism and economic determinism. Society, whether generalized as such or as 'capitalist society' or as 'the social and cultural forms of the capitalist mode of production', is seen as the primarily negative force which follows from any understanding of determination as only the setting of limits. But 'society', or 'the historical event', can never in such ways be categorically abstracted from 'individuals' and 'individual wills'. Such a separation leads straight to an alienated, objectivist 'society', working 'unconsciously', and to comprehension of individuals as 'pre-social' or even anti-social. 'The individual' or 'the genotype' then become positive extra-social forces.

This is where the full concept of determination is crucial. For in practice determination is never only the setting of limits; it is also the exertion of pressures. As it happens this is also a sense of 'determine' in English: to determine or be determined to do something is an act of will and purpose. In a whole social process, these positive determinations, which may be experienced individually but which are always social acts, indeed often specific social formations, have very complex relations with the negative determinations that are experienced as limits. For they are by no means only pressures against the limits, though these are crucially important. They are at least as often pressures derived from the formation and momentum of a given social mode: in effect a compulsion to act in ways that maintain and renew it. They are also, and vitally, pressures exerted by new formations, with their as yet unrealized intentions and demands. 'Society' is then never only the 'dead husk' which limits social and individual fulfilment. It is always also a constitutive process with very powerful pressures which are both expressed in political, economic, and cultural formations and, to take the full weight of 'constitutive', are internalized and become 'individual wills'. Determination of this whole kind—a complex and interrelated process of limits and pressures—is in the whole social process itself and nowhere else: not in an abstracted 'mode of production' nor in an abstracted 'psychology'. Any abstraction of determinism, based on the isolation of autonomous categories, which are seen as controlling or which

can be used for prediction, is then a mystification of the specific
and always related determinants which are the real social process—an active and conscious as well as, by default, a passive
and objectified historical experience.

The concept of 'overdetermination' is an attempt to avoid the
isolation of autonomous *categories* but at the same time to
emphasize relatively autonomous yet of course interactive *practices*. In its most positive forms—that is, in its recognition of
multiple forces, rather than the isolated forces of modes or
techniques of production, and in its further recognition of these
forces as structured, in particular historical situations, rather
than elements of an ideal totality or, worse, merely adja-
cent—the concept of 'overdetermination' is more useful than
any other as a way of understanding historically lived situations
and the authentic complexities of practice. It is especially useful
as a way of understanding 'contradictions' and the ordinary
version of 'the dialectic', which can so easily be abstracted as
features of a theoretically isolated (determining) situation or
movement, which is then expected to develop according to
certain (determinist) laws. In any whole society, both the relative autonomy and the relative unevenness of different practices
(forms of practical consciousness) decisively affect actual
development, and affect it, in the sense of pressures and limits,
as determinants. Yet there are also difficulties in the concept. It
was used by Freud to indicate the structured multiple causation
of a *symptom*: a crystallization very similar to the Frankfurt
School's concept of a *dialectical image* (see p. 103). Some traces
of this origin survive in some of its theoretical uses (e.g. in
Althusser, who introduced it in Marxism but who failed to apply
its most positive elements to his own work on ideology). As with
'determination', so 'overdetermination' can be abstracted to a
structure (symptom), which then, if in complex ways, 'develops'
(forms, holds, breaks down) by the laws of its internal structural
relations. As a form of analysis this is often effective, but in its
isolation of the structure it can shift attention from the real
location of all practice and practical consciousness: 'the practical activity . . . the practical process of development of men'.
Any categorical objectification of determined or overdetermined
structures is a repetition of the basic error of 'economism' at a
more serious level, since it now offers to subsume (at times with
a certain arrogance) all lived, practical and unevenly formed and

formative experience. One of the reasons for this error, whether in economism or in an alternative structuralism, is a misunderstanding of the nature of 'productive forces'.

3. Productive Forces

Underlying any argument about 'base' and 'superstructure', or about the nature of 'determination', is a decisive concept: that of 'productive forces'. It is a very important concept in Marx, and in all subsequent Marxism. But it is also a variable concept, and the variations have been exceptionally important for Marxist cultural theory.

The central difficulty is that all the key words—produce, product, production, productive—went through a specialized development in the course of the development of capitalism. Thus to analyse capitalism was at once to see it as a distinct process of 'production' and to refer it to a general process, of which it is a particular historical kind. The difficulty is that the general process is still most readily defined in the specific and limiting terms of capitalist production. Marx was perfectly clear about the distinction between 'production in general' and 'capitalist production'. Indeed it was the claim of the latter, through its political economy, to the universality of its own specific and historical conditions, that he especially attacked. But the history had happened, in the language as in so much else. What is then profoundly difficult is that Marx analysed 'capitalist production' in and through its own terms, and at the same time, whether looking to the past or the future, was in effect compelled to use many of the same terms for more general or historically different processes. As he himself wrote:

'Production in general' is an abstraction, but it is a rational abstraction, in so far as it singles out and fixes the common features, thereby saving us repetition. Yet these general or common features discovered by comparison constitute something very complex, whose constituent elements have different destinations. . . . All the stages of production have certain destinations in common, which we generalize in thought: but the so-called general conditions of all production are nothing but abstract conceptions which do not go to make up any real stage in the history of production. (Grundrisse, 85)

It must be added that the concept of 'material production' is similarly abstract, but also similarly rational for particular purposes. As an abstraction (for example, in bourgeois political economy) it can be separated from other categories such as consumption, distribution, and exchange; and all these can be separated both from the social relations, the form of society, within which they are specifically and variably interrelating activities, and, further, from the personal activities which are their only concrete modes of existence. But in capitalist society 'material production' is a specific form, determined and understood in the forms of capital, wage-labour, and the production of commodities. That this 'material production' has itself been produced, by the social development of particular forms of production, is then the first thing to realize if we are trying to understand the nature of even this production, in which, because of actual historical developments,

material life generally appears as the aim while the production of this material life, labour (which is now the only possible but . . . negative form of personal activity) appears as the means. (GI, 66)

Moreover, in capitalist society

The productive forces appear to be completely independent and severed from the individuals and to constitute a self-subsistent world alongside the individuals. (GI, 65)

What then is a 'productive force'? It is all and any of the means of the production and reproduction of real life. It may be seen as a particular kind of agricultural or industrial production, but any such kind is already a certain mode of social co-operation and the application and development of a certain body of social knowledge. The production of this specific social co-operation or of this specific social knowledge is itself carried through by productive forces. In all our activities in the world we produce not only the satisfaction of our needs but new needs and new definitions of needs. Fundamentally, in this human historical process, we produce ourselves and our societies, and it is within these developing and variable forms that 'material production', then itself variable, both in mode and scope, is itself carried on.

But if this is really Marx's basic position, how did it happen that a more limited definition of 'productive forces', and with it a separation and abstraction of 'material production' and the 'material' or 'economic' 'base', came not only to predominate in Marxism but to be taken, by almost everyone else, as defining it. One reason is the course of a particular argument. It was not

Marxism, but the systems with which it contended and continues to contend, which had separated and abstracted various parts of this whole social process. It was the assertion and explanation of political forms and philosophical and general ideas as independent of, 'above', the material social process, that produced a necessary kind of counter-assertion. In the flow of polemic this was often overstated, until it came to repeat, in a simple reversal of terms, the kind of error it attacked.

But there are deeper reasons than this. If you live in a capitalist society, it is capitalist forms that you must analyse. Marx lived, and we live, in a society in which indeed 'the productive forces appear to . . . constitute a self-subsistent world'. Thus in analysing the operation of productive forces which are not only perceived as, but in central ways really are, of this kind, it is easy, within the only available language, to slip into describing them as if they were universal and general, and as if certain 'laws' of their relations to other activities were fundamental truths. Marxism thus often took the colouring of a specifically bourgeois and capitalist kind of materialism. It could isolate 'productive forces' as 'industry' (even at times as 'heavy industry'), and here again the evidence of language is significant. It was in the 'Industrial Revolution' that 'industry' changed from being a word which described the human activity of assiduous effort and application to a word which predominantly describes productive institutions: a 'self-subsistent world'. Of course these were capitalist institutions, and 'production' itself was eventually subordinated to the capitalist element, as now in descriptions of the 'entertainment industry' or the 'holiday industry'. The practical subordination of all human activities (with a saving clause for certain activities which were called 'personal' or 'aesthetic') to the modes and norms of capitalist institutions became more and more effective. Marxists, insisting on this and protesting against it, were caught in a practical ambivalence. The insistence, in effect, diluted the protest. It is then often said that the insistence was 'too materialist', a 'vulgar materialism'. But the truth is that it was never materialist enough.

What any notion of a 'self-subsistent order' suppresses is the material character of the productive forces which produce such a version of production. Indeed it is often a way of suppressing full consciousness of the very nature of such a society. If 'production', in capitalist society, is the production of commodities for a market, then different but misleading terms are found for every other kind of production and productive force. What is most often suppressed is the direct material production of 'politics'. Yet any ruling class devotes a significant part of material production to establishing a political order. The social and political order which maintains a capitalist market, like the social and political struggles which created it, is necessarily a material production. From castles and palaces and churches to prisons and workhouses and schools; from weapons of war to a controlled press: any ruling class, in variable ways though always materially, produces a social and political order. These are never superstructural activities. They are the necessary material production within which an apparently self-subsistent mode of production can alone be carried on. The complexity of this process is especially remarkable in advanced capitalist societies, where it is wholly beside the point to isolate 'production' and 'industry' from the comparably material production of 'defence', 'law and order', 'welfare', 'entertainment', and 'public opinion'. In failing to grasp the material character of the production of a social and political order, this specialized (and bourgeois) materialism failed also, but even more conspicuously, to understand the material character of the production of a cultural order. The concept of the 'superstructure' was then not a reduction but an evasion.

Yet the difficulty is that if we reject the idea of a 'self-subsistent world' of productive (industrial) forces, and describe productive forces as all and any activities in the social process as a whole, we have made a necessary critique but, at least in the first instance, lost edge and specificity. To go beyond this difficulty will be a matter for later argument; we have first to specify the negative effects, in cultural analysis, of the specialized version of 'productive forces' and 'production'. We can best specify them in Marx himself, rather than in the many later examples. There is a footnote in the *Grundrisse* in which it is argued that a piano-maker is a productive worker, engaged in productive labour, but that a pianist is not, since his labour is not labour which reproduces capital. The extraordinary inadequacy of this distinction to advanced capitalism, in which the production of music (and not just its instruments) is an important branch of capitalist production, may be only an occasion for updating. But the real error is more fundamental.

In his sustained and brilliant analysis of capitalist society, Marx was working both with and beyond the categories of bourgeois political economy. His distinction of 'productive labour' was in fact developed, in this note, from Adam Smith. It still makes sense (or can be revised to make sense) in those bourgeois terms. Production is then work on raw materials to make commodities, which enter the capitalist system of distribution and exchange. Thus a piano is a commodity; music is (or was) not. At this level, in an analysis of capitalism, there is no great difficulty until we see that a necessary result is the projection (alienation) of a whole body of activities which have to be isolated as 'the realm of art and ideas', as 'aesthetics', as 'ideology', or, less flatteringly, as 'the superstructure'. None of these can then be grasped as they are; as real practices, elements of a whole material social process; not a realm or a world or a superstructure, but many and variable productive practices, with specific conditions and intentions. To fail to see this is not only to lose contact with the actuality of these practices, as has repeatedly occurred in forms of analysis derived from the terms of this specialized (industrial) materialism. It is to begin the whole difficult process of discovering and describing relations between all these practices, and between them and the other practices which have been isolated as 'production', as 'the base', or as the 'self-subsistent world', in an extremely awkward and disabling position. It is indeed to begin this most difficult kind of work head down and standing on one foot. Such feats of agility are not impossible, and have indeed been performed. But it would be more reasonable to get back on both feet again, and to look at our actual productive activities without assuming in advance that only some of them are material.

4. From Reflection to Mediation

The usual consequence of the base–superstructure formula, with its specialized and limited interpretations of productive forces and of the process of determination, is a description—even at times a theory—of art and thought as 'reflection'. The metaphor of 'reflection' has a long history in the analysis of art and ideas. Yet the physical process and relationship that it implies have proved compatible with several radically different theories. Thus art can be said to 'reflect the real world', holding 'the mirror up to nature', but every term of such a definition has been in protracted and necessary dispute. Art can be seen as reflecting not 'mere appearances' but the 'reality' behind these: the 'inner nature' of the world, or its 'constitutive forms'. Or art is seen as reflecting not the 'lifeless world', but the world as seen in the mind of the artist. The elaboration and sophistication of arguments of these kinds are remarkable.

Materialism appears to constitute a fundamental challenge to them. If the real world is material, it can indeed be seen in its constitutive forms, but these will not be metaphysical, and reflection will be necessarily of a material reality. This can lead to the concept of 'false' or 'distorted' reflection, in which something (metaphysics, 'ideology') prevents true reflection. Similarly, the 'mind of the artist' can be seen as itself materially conditioned; its reflection is then not independent but itself a material function.

Two versions of this materialism became dominant in Marxist thinking. First, there was the interpretation of consciousness as mere 'reflexes, echoes, phantoms, and sublimates'; this was discussed in relation to one of the concepts of ideology. But as a necessary complement to this reductive account, an alternative interpretation of consciousness as 'scientific truth', based on real knowledge of the material world, was strongly emphasized. This alternative could be extended relatively easily to include accounts of 'knowledge' and 'thought', but for obvious reasons it left 'art' relatively neglected and exposed. Within this version the most common account of art was then a positivist theory, in which the metaphor of 'reflection' played a central role. The true function of art was defined in terms of 'realism' or less often 'naturalism'—both nineteenth-century terms themselves much affected by related concepts of science. Art reflected reality; if it did not it was false or unimportant. And what was reality? The 'production and reproduction of real life', now commonly described as 'the base', with art part of its 'superstructure'. The ambiguity is then obvious. A doctrine about the real world expressed in the materialism of objects leads to one kind of theory of art: showing the objects (including human actions as objects) 'as they really are'. But this can be maintained, in its simplest form, only by knowing 'the base' as an object: the development already discussed. To know the 'base' as a process at once complicates the object–reflection model which had appeared so powerful.

This complication was fought out in rival definitions of 'realism' and 'naturalism'. Each term had begun as a secular and radical emphasis on human social knowledge. Naturalism was an alternative to supernaturalism; realism to a deliberately falsifying ('romanticizing', 'mythmaking', 'prettifying') art. Yet the enclosure of each concept within a special doctrine of 'the object as it really is' reduced their radical challenge. The making of art was incorporated into a static, objectivist doctrine, within which 'reality', 'the real world', 'the base', could be *separately* known, by the criteria of scientific truth, and their 'reflections' in art then judged by their conformity or lack of conformity with them: in fact with their positivist versions.

It was at this point that a different materialist theory became necessary. For it was only in very simple cases that the object–reflection model could be actually illustrated or verified. Moreover, there was already a crucial distinction between 'mechanical materialism'—seeing the world as objects and excluding activity—and 'historical materialism'—seeing the material life process as human activity. The simplest theories of 'reflection' were based on a mechanical materialism. But a different account appeared possible if 'the real world', instead of being isolated as an object, was grasped as a material social *process*, with certain inherent qualities and tendencies. As earlier in idealism, but now with altered specification, art could be seen as reflecting not separated objects and superficial events but the essential forces and movements underlying them. This was in turn made the basis for distinction between 'realism' (dynamic) and 'naturalism' (static).

Yet it is quickly evident that this is radically incompatible with any doctrine of 'reflection', except in one special and influential adaptation. The movement from abstract objectivism to this sense of objectified process was decisive. But the sense of objectified process can be almost at once rendered back to its original abstract and objectivist condition, by a definition of the already known (scientifically discoverd and attested) 'laws' of this process. Art can then be defined as 'reflecting' these laws. What is already *and otherwise* known as the basic reality of the material social process is reflected, of course in its own ways, by art. If it is not (and the test is available, by comparison of this given knowledge of reality with any actual art produced), then it is a case of distortion, falsification, or superficiality: not art but ideology. Rash extensions were then possible to new categorical distinctions: not progressive art but reactionary art; not socialist art but bourgeois or capitalist art; not art but mass culture; and so on almost indefinitely. The decisive theory of art as reflection, not now of objects but of real and verifiable social and historical processes, was thus extensively maintained and elaborated. The theory became at once a cultural programme and a critical school.

It has of course been heavily attacked from older and often more substantial positions. It has been widely identified as a damaging consequence of a materialist outlook. But once again, what is wrong with the theory is that it is not materialist enough. The most damaging consequence of any theory of art as reflection is that, through its persuasive physical metaphor (in which a reflection simply occurs, within the physical properties of light, when an object or movement is brought into relation with a reflective surface—the mirror and then the mind), it succeeds in suppressing the actual work on material—in a final sense, the material social process—which is the making of any art work. By projecting and alienating this material process to 'reflection', the social and material character of artistic activity—of that art-work which is at once 'material' and 'imaginative'—was suppressed. It was at this point that the idea of reflection was challenged by the idea of 'mediation'.

'Mediation' was intended to describe an active process. Its predominant general sense had been an act of intercession, reconciliation, or interpretation between adversaries or strangers. In idealist philosophy it had been a concept of reconciliation between opposites, within a totality. A more neutral sense had also developed, for interaction between separate forces. The distinction between 'mediate' and 'immediate' had been developed to emphasize 'mediation' as an *indirect* connection or agency between separate kinds of act.

It is then easy to see the attraction of 'mediation' as a term to describe the process of relationship between 'society' and 'art', or between 'the base' and 'the superstructure'. We should not expect to find (or always to find) directly 'reflected' social realities in art, since these (often or always) pass through a process of 'mediation' in which their original content is changed. This general proposition, however, can be understood in several different ways. The change involved in mediation can be simply a matter of indirect expression: the social realities are 'projected' or 'disguised', and to recover them is a process of working back through the mediation to their original forms. Relying mainly on the concept of 'ideology' as (class-based) distortion, this kind of reductive analysis, and of 'stripping', 'laying bare' or 'unmasking', has been common in Marxist work. If we remove the elements of mediation, an area of reality, and then also of the ideological elements which distorted its perception or which determined its presentation, will become clear. (In our own time this sense of mediation has been especially applied to 'the media', which are assumed to distort and present 'reality' in ideological ways.)

Yet this negative sense of 'mediation', which has been heavily supported by psychoanalytical concepts such as 'repression' and 'sublimation', and by 'rationalization' in a sense close to the negative sense of 'ideology', has coexisted with a sense which offers to be positive. This is especially the contribution of the Frankfurt School. Here the change involved in 'mediation' is not necessarily seen as distortion or disguise. Rather, all active relations between different kinds of being and consciousness are inevitably mediated, and this process is not a separable agency—a 'medium'—but intrinsic to the properties of the related kinds. "Mediation is in the object itself, not something between the object and that to which it is brought."[*] Thus mediation is a positive process in social reality, rather than a

---

[*] T. W. Adorno, 'Thesen zur Kunstsoziologie', *Kölner Zeitschrift für Soziologie und Sozialpsychologie*, xix, 1 (March 1967).

process added to it by way of projection, disguise, or interpretation.

It is difficult to be sure how much is gained by substituting the metaphor of 'mediation' for the metaphor of 'reflection'. On the one hand it goes beyond the passivity of reflection theory; it indicates an active process, of some kind. On the other hand, in almost all cases, it perpetuates a basic dualism. Art does not reflect social reality, the superstructure does not reflect the base, *directly*; culture is a mediation of society. But it is virtually impossible to sustain the metaphor of 'mediation' (*Vermittlung*) without some sense of separate and pre-existent areas or orders of reality, between which the mediating process occurs whether independently or as determined by their prior natures. Within the inheritance of idealist philosophy the process is usually, in practice, seen as a mediation between categories, which have been assumed to be distinct. Mediation, in this range of use, then seems little more than a sophistication of reflection.

Yet the underlying problem is obvious. If 'reality' and 'speaking about reality' (the 'material social process' and 'language') are taken as categorically distinct, concepts such as 'reflection' and 'mediation' are inevitable. The same pressure can be observed in attempts to interpret the Marxist phrase 'the production and reproduction of real life' as if production were the primary social (economic) process and 'reproduction' its 'symbolic' or 'signifying' or 'cultural' counterpart. Such attempts are either alternatives to the Marxist emphasis on an inherent and constitutive 'practical consciousness', or, at their best, ways of specifying its actual operations. The problem is different, from the beginning, if we see language and signification as indissoluble elements of the material social process itself, involved all the time both in production and reproduction. The forms of actual displacement and alienation experienced in class societies have led to recurrent concepts of isolated relations between 'separate' orders: 'reflection' from idealist thought through naturalism to a positivist kind of Marxism; 'mediation' from religious thought through idealist philosophy to Hegelian variants of Marxism. To the extent that it indicates an active and substantial process, 'mediation' is always the less alienated concept. In its modern development it approaches the sense of inherent constitutive consciousness, and is in any case important as an alternative to simple reductionism, in which every real act or work is methodically rendered back to an assumed primary category, usually specified (self-specified) as 'concrete reality'. But when the process of mediation is seen as positive and substantial, as a necessary process of the making of meanings and values, in the necessary form of the general social process of signification and communication, it is really only a hindrance to describe it as 'mediation' at all. For the metaphor takes us back to the very concept of the 'intermediary' which, at its best, this constitutive and constituting sense rejects.

5. Typification and Homology

One important way of restating the idea of 'reflection', and of giving particular substance to the idea of 'mediation, is to be found in the concept of 'typicality'. This was already important in nineteenth-century thought, in two general forms. First, there was the concept, as in Taine, of the 'ideal' type: a definition normally attached to 'heroes' in literature, who were seen as "the important characters, the elementary forces, the deepest layers of human nature". This is a very traditional definition, with obvious reference back to Aristotle, in which the notion of typicality is in effect a rendering of 'universals': the permanently important elements of human nature and the human condition. While it seems natural to associate 'universals' with religious, metaphysical, or idealist forms of thought, it can also be argued that permanent elements of the human social situation, always of course modified by specific historical situations, are 'typical' or 'universal' in a more secular sense. The social, historical, and evolutionary dimensions of human nature can be expressed, in secular terms, as distinct both from idealism and from a non-historical or non-evolutionary 'sociologism'. Lukács's (trans-formed-Hegelian) concept of 'world-historical individuals' is an example of 'type' in this sense.

A different emphasis, specifically associated with new doctrines of realism, was made by Belinsky, Chernyshevsky, and Dobrolyubov, and became influential in Marxism. Here the 'typical' is the fully 'characteristic' or fully 'representative' character or situation: the specific figure from which we can reasonably extrapolate; or, to put it the other way round, the specific figure which concentrates and intensifies a much more general reality. It is then easy to see how the notion of 'reflection' can be redefined in ways that appear to overcome its most obvious limitations. It is not the 'mere surface', or 'appearances only', which are reflected in art, but the 'essential' or 'underlying' or 'general' reality, and this as an intrinsic process, rather than as a separated process in time. It must then of course be observed that 'reflection' is an extremely odd way of describing the processes of intrinsic concentration which this new sense indicates. But the amendment permitted the continuation of general statements to the effect that 'art reflects social reality', while specifying its detailed processes in more figurative (selective or intensifying) ways.

Indeed only one element needed to be added to make this an influential Marxist theory of art: the insistence that 'social reality' is a *dynamic* process, and that it is this *movement* that is reflected by 'typification'. Art, by figurative means, typifies "the elements and tendencies of reality that recur according to regular laws, although changing with the changing circumstances" (Lukács). The description of social reality as a dynamic process is then a major advance, but this is qualified, and in one sense nullified, by the familiar and ominous reference to 'laws'. There is an obvious danger of reducing this theory to art as the typification (representation, illustration) not of the dynamic process but of its ('known') laws. In metaphysical and idealist thought a comparable theory had included not only recognition of the essential but through this recognition an indication of its desirability or inevitability, according to the basic laws of reality. Similarly, one common form of this Marxist theory indicated not only recognition of (social and historical) reality but also a demonstration of its inevitable (and desirable) movements, according to the (scientific) laws of history and society. Indeed, in one tendency, that of 'socialist realism', the concept of the 'ideal type' took on connotations of the 'future man'. Any of these positions can be defended, but the concept of 'typicality' is intolerably confused by their variety.

In general terms the sense of 'typicality' most consonant with Marxism is that based on recognition of a constitutive and constituting process of social and historical reality, which is then specifically expressed in some particular 'type'. This related movement, of recognition and means of specific expression, is one of the most common serious senses of 'mediation', in spite of the basic disadvantages of that term. But 'type' can still be understood in two radically different ways: as an 'emblem' or 'symbol', or as the representative example of a significant classification. It is the latter sense that has been predominant in Marxist thinking (even where qualified by recognitions of 'emblematic' or 'symbolic' art as authentic in terms of a broadened sense of 'representation' and 'significance'). There is a persistent presupposition of a knowable (often wholly knowable) reality in terms of which the typification will be recognized and indeed (in a normal process in 'Marxist criticism') verified. This pre-supposition repeats, if in more complex and at times very sophisticated forms, the basic dualism of all theories centred on the concept of 'reflection' or, in its ordinary sense, 'mediation', or, we can now add, the ordinary sense of 'typification'.

In the later work of the Frankfurt School, and in a different way in the work of Marxist structuralists, other concepts were developed: notably that of 'correspondences', which has some interesting relations with one variation of 'type'; and the radically new concept of 'homology'.

The strict notion of 'correspondences' is at the opposite pole from 'typicality'. Walter Benjamin, taking the term from Baudelaire, used it to describe 'an experience which seeks to establish itself in crisis-proof form. This is possible only within the realm of the ritual.' * The actual process of the making of art is then the crystallization of such experiences, by such methods. Its presence and its authenticity can be recognized by what Benjamin called its 'aura'. Such a definition can be held at a simple subjectivist level, or it can be moved towards the familiar abstractions of 'myth', of the 'collective unconscious' or of 'the creative imagination'. Benjamin moved it in these ways, but he extended it also, and crucially, to 'the historical process', in particular relation to his awareness of the changing social and material conditions of different kinds of actual art-work. Meanwhile, more generally, the Frankfurt School was developing the idea of 'dialectical images' as crystallizations of the historical process. This concept is very near one sense of 'type', giving a new social and historical sense of 'emblematic' or 'symbolic' art.

The idea of 'dialectical images' obviously needs definition. Adorno complained that, in Benjamin's hands, they were often in effect 'reflections of social reality', reduced to 'simple facticity'. 'Dialectical images', he went on to argue, 'are models not of social products, but rather objective constellations in which the social condition represents itself'. They can 'never be expected to be an ideological or in general a social "product"'. This argument depends on a distinction between 'the real social process' and the various fixed forms, in 'ideology' or 'social products', which merely appear to represent or express it. The real social process is always mediated, and one of the positive forms of such mediation is the genuine 'dialectical image'.

* *Zeitschrift für Sozialforschung*, v, 1, Frankfort, 1936.

There is of course still a problem in the description of all inherent and constitutive consciousness as 'mediated', even when this mediation is recognized as itself inherent. Yet in other respects this is a crucial step towards the recognition of art as a primary process. Yet this also was what Benjamin wished to argue, except that, relying less on the categorical priority of 'mediation', he sought to lay one kind of process beside another, and to explore their relations, in what has really to be seen as the exploration of 'correspondences' (connections) in a much more literal and familiar sense.

What then, theoretically, are such correspondences, and what is their relation to the apparently more rigorous concept of 'homology'? At one level correspondences are resemblances, in seemingly very different specific practices, which may be shown by analysis to be both direct and directly related expressions of and responses to a general social process. There is an example in Benjamin's surprising but convincing configuration of the ragpickers, the 'bohemians', and the new poetic methods of Paris under the Second Empire. Characteristically all the evidence adduced for these resemblances is highly specific. It is centred in Baudelaire's poem The Ragpickers' Wine, but extends to a wide range of new kinds of activity in the extraordinary commercial expansion of the city. Then at another level correspondences are not so much resemblances as analogies, as in the case of the figure of the city stroller and the corresponding forms of mobile and detached observation in panoramic journalism, in the detective story, and in the poetry of isolation within the city crowd. This evidence is again direct and specific, but what it supports is a correspondence of observational perspective, and thence of literary stance, in different social and literary forms. At another level again, correspondences are neither resemblances nor analogies but displaced connections, as in Adorno's example of the (negative) relation between Viennese 'number games' (from a new tonal system in music to logical positivism) and the (backward) state of Austrian material development, given its intellectual and technical capacities. Here, while the immediate evidence is direct, the plausibility of the relation depends not only on a formal analysis of the historical social process but on the consequent deduction of a displacement or even an absence.

Any of these levels may be loosely described as 'homology', but this concept itself has a significant range. It extends from a sense of resemblance to one of analogy, in directly observable terms, but it includes also, and more influentially, a sense of corresponding *forms* or *structures*, which are necessarily the results of different kinds of analysis. The concept of 'homology' was developed in the life sciences, where it included a radical distinction from 'analogy'. 'Homology' is correspondence in origin and development, 'analogy' in appearance and function. The related distinction between 'structure' and 'function' is directly relevant. There is then a range from 'general homology' (the relation of an organ to a general type) through 'serial homology' (related orders of connection) to 'special homology' (the correspondence of a part of one organism to another part of another organism). Extension of these senses to social or cultural analysis is suggestive but usually itself analogical.

The radical distinction between variants of 'correspondence' and 'homology', in cultural analysis, must be related to the fundamental theoretical distinctions that have already been examined. Thus 'correspondence' and 'homology' can be sophisticated variants of a theory of reflection, or of 'mediation' in its dualist sense. A cultural phenomenon acquires its full significance only when it is seen as a form of (known or knowable) general social process or structure. The distinction between process and structure is then crucial. Resemblances and analogies between different specific practices are usually relations *within* a process, working inwards from particular forms to a general form. Displaced connections, and the important idea of *homologous structures*, depend less on an immediately observable process than on an effectively completed historical and social structural analysis, in which a general form has become apparent, and specific instances of this form can be discovered, not so much or even at all in content, but in specific and autonomous but finally related forms.

These distinctions have considerable practical importance. Both 'correspondence' and 'homology', in certain senses, can be modes of exploration and analysis of a social process which is grasped from the beginning as a complex of specific but related activities. Selection is evidently involved, but as a matter of principle there is no *a priori* distinction between the necessary and the contingent, the 'social' and the 'cultural', the 'base' and the 'superstructure'. Correspondence and homology are then not formal but specific relations: examples of real social relationships, in their variable practice, which have common forms of origin. Or again, 'correspondence' and 'homology' can be seen as forms of the 'typical': crystallizations, in superficially unrelated fields, of a social process which is nowhere fully represented but which is specifically present, in determinate forms, in a range of different works and activities.

On the other hand, 'correspondence' and 'homology' can be in effect restatements of the base—superstructure model and of the 'determinist' sense of determination. Analysis begins from a known structure of society, or a known movement of history. Specific analysis then discovers examples of this movement or structure in cultural works. Or, where 'correspondence' seems to indicate too simple an idea of reflection, analysis is directed towards instances of formal or structural homology between a social order, its ideology, and its cultural forms. Very important work (that of Goldmann, for example) has been done in this last mode. But the practical and theoretical problems it raises are severe. The most evident practical effect is an extreme selectivity. Only the cultural evidence which fits the homology is directly introduced. Other evidence is neglected, often with the explanation that the homologous *is* the significant evidence, and indeed is a way of distinguishing 'great works' from others. Theoretically the problem is that the 'social order'—here a formal term for social and historical process—has to be given an initially structured form, and the most available form is 'ideology' or 'world-view', which is already evidently but abstractly structured. This procedure is repeated in the cultural analysis itself, for the homological analysis is now not of 'content' but of 'form', and the cultural process is not its active practices but its formal products or objects. The 'fit' or homology between 'ideology' and 'cultural object', thus formally conceived, is often striking and important. But a heavy price is paid. First, empirically, in the procedural selectivity of historical and cultural evidence. The substitution of *epochal* for connected historical analysis is especially characteristic of this method. Second, practically, in the understanding of contemporary cultural process. None of the dualist theories, expressed as reflection or mediation, and none of the formalist and structuralist theories, expressed in variants of correspondence or homology, can be fully carried through to contemporary practice, since in different ways they all depend on a *known* history, a known *structure*, known *products*. Analytic relations can be handled in this way; practical relations hardly at all.

An alternative approach to the same problems, but one which is more directly oriented to cultural process and to practical relations, can be found in the developing concept of 'hegemony'.

6. Hegemony

The traditional definition of 'hegemony' is political rule or domination, especially in relations between states. Marxism extended the definition of rule or domination to relations between social classes, and especially to definitions of a *ruling class*. 'Hegemony' then acquired a further significant sense in the work of Antonio Gramsci, carried out under great difficulties in a Fascist prison between 1927 and 1935. Much is still uncertain in Gramsci's use of the concept, but his work is one of the major turning-points in Marxist cultural theory.

Gramsci made a distinction between 'rule' (*dominio*) and 'hegemony'. 'Rule' is expressed in directly political forms and in times of crisis by direct or effective coercion. But the more normal situation is a complex interlocking of political, social, and cultural forces, and 'hegemony', according to different interpretations, is either this or the active social and cultural forces which are its necessary elements. Whatever the implications of the concept for Marxist political theory (which has still to recognize many kinds of direct political control, social class control, and economic control, as well as this more general formation), the effects on cultural theory are immediate. For 'hegemony' is a concept which at once includes and goes beyond two powerful earlier concepts: that of 'culture' as a 'whole social process', in which men define and shape their whole lives; and that of 'ideology', in any of its Marxist senses, in which a system of meanings and values is the expression or projection of a particular class interest.

'Hegemony' goes beyond 'culture', as previously defined, in its insistence on relating the 'whole social process' to specific distributions of power and influence. To say that 'men' define and shape their whole lives is true only in abstraction. In any actual society there are specific inequalities in means and therefore in capacity to realize this process. In a class society these are primarily inequalities between classes. Gramsci therefore introduced the necessary recognition of dominance and subordination in what has still, however, to be recognized as a whole process.

It is in just this recognition of the *wholeness* of the process that the concept of 'hegemony' goes beyond 'ideology'. What is decisive is not only the conscious system of ideas and beliefs, but the whole lived social process as practically organized by specific and dominant meanings and values. Ideology, in its normal senses, is a relatively formal and articulated system of meanings, values, and beliefs, of a kind that can be abstracted as a 'worldview' or a 'class outlook'. This explains its popularity as a concept in retrospective analysis (in base–superstructure models or in homology), since a system of ideas can be abstracted from that once living social process and represented, usually by the selection of 'leading' or typical 'ideologists' or 'ideological features', as the decisive form in which consciousness was at once expressed and controlled (or, as in Althusser, was in effect unconscious, as an imposed structure). The relatively mixed, confused, incomplete, or inarticulate consciousness of actual men in that period and society is thus overridden in the name of this decisive generalized system, and indeed in structural homology is procedurally excluded as peripheral or ephemeral. It is the fully articulate and systematic forms which are recognizable as ideology, and there is a corresponding tendency in the analysis of art to look only for similarly fully articulate and systematic expressions of this ideology in the content (base–superstructure) or form (homology) of actual works. In less selective procedures, less dependent on the inherent classicism of the definition of form as fully articulate and systematic, the tendency is to consider works as variants of, or as variably affected by, the decisive abstracted ideology.

More generally, this sense of 'an ideology' is applied in abstract ways to the actual consciousness of both dominant and subordinated classes. A dominant class 'has' this ideology in relatively pure and simple forms. A subordinate class has, in one version, *nothing but* this ideology as its consciousness (since the production of all ideas is, by axiomatic definition, in the hands of those who control the primary means of production) or, in another version, has this ideology imposed on its otherwise different consciousness, which it must struggle to sustain or develop against 'ruling-class ideology'.

The concept of hegemony often, in practice, resembles these definitions, but it is distinct in its refusal to equate consciousness with the articulate formal system which can be and ordinarily is abstracted as 'ideology'. It of course does not exclude the articulate and formal meanings, values and beliefs which a dominant class develops and propagates. But it does not equate these with consciousness, or rather it does not reduce consciousness to them. Instead it sees the relations of domination and subordination, in their forms as practical consciousness, as in effect a saturation of the whole process of living—not only of political and economic activity, nor only of manifest social activity, but of the whole substance of lived identities and relationships, to such a depth that the pressures and limits of what can ultimately be seen as a specific economic, political, and cultural system seem to most of us the pressures and limits of simple experience and common sense. Hegemony is then not only the articulate upper level of 'ideology', nor are its forms of control only those ordinarily seen as 'manipulation' or 'indoctrination'. It is a whole body of practices and expectations, over the whole of living: our senses and assignments of energy, our shaping perceptions of ourselves and our world. It is a lived system of meanings and values—constitutive and constituting—which as they are experienced as practices appear as reciprocally confirming. It thus constitutes a sense of reality for most people in the society, a sense of absolute because experienced reality beyond which it is very difficult for most members of the society to move, in most areas of their lives. It is, that is to say, in the strongest sense a 'culture', but a culture which has also to be seen as the lived dominance and subordination of particular classes.

There are two immediate advantages in this concept of hegemony. First, its forms of domination and subordination correspond much more closely to the normal processes of social organization and control in developed societies than the more familiar projections from the idea of a ruling class, which are usually based on much earlier and simpler historical phases. It can speak, for example, to the realities of electoral democracy, and to the significant modern areas of 'leisure' and 'private life', more specifically and more actively than older ideas of domination, with their trivializing explanations of simple 'manipulation', 'corruption', and 'betrayal'. If the pressures and limits of a given form of domination are to this extent experienced *and in practice internalized*, the whole question of class rule, and of opposition to it, is transformed. Gramsci's emphasis on the creation of an alternative hegemony, by the practical connection of many different forms of struggle, including those not easily recognizable as and indeed not primarily 'political' and 'economic', thus leads to a much more profound and more active sense of revolutionary activity in a highly developed society than the persistently abstract models derived from very different historical situations. The sources of any alternative hegemony are indeed difficult to define. For Gramsci they spring from the working class, but not this class as an ideal or abstract construction. What he sees, rather, is a working people which has, precisely, to become a class, and a potentially hegemonic class, against the pressures and limits of an existing and powerful hegemony.

Second, and more immediately in this context, there is a whole different way of seeing cultural activity, both as tradition and as practice. Cultural work and activity are not now, in any ordinary sense, a superstructure: not only because of the depth and thoroughness at which any cultural hegemony is lived, but because cultural tradition and practice are seen as much more than superstructural expressions—reflections, mediations, or typifications—of a formed social and economic structure. On the contrary, they are among the basic processes of the formation itself and, further, related to a much wider area of reality than the abstractions of 'social' and 'economic' experience. People seeing themselves and each other in directly personal relationships; people seeing the natural world and themselves in it; people using their physical and material resources for what one kind of society specializes to 'leisure' and 'entertainment' and 'art': all these active experiences and practices, which make up so much of the reality of a culture and its cultural production can be seen as they are, without reduction to other categories of content, and without the characteristic straining to fit them (directly as reflection, indirectly as mediation or typification or analogy) to other and determining manifest economic and political relationships. Yet they can still be seen as elements of a hegemony: an inclusive social and cultural formation which indeed to be effective has to extend to and include, indeed to form and be formed from, this whole area of lived experience.

Many difficulties then arise, both theoretically and practically, but it is important to recognize how many blind alleys we may now be saved from entering. If any lived culture is necessarily so extensive, the problems of domination and subordination on the one hand, and of the extraordinary complexity of any actual cultural tradition and practice on the other, can at last be directly approached.

There is of course the difficulty that domination and subordination, as effective descriptions of cultural formation, will, by many, be refused; that the alternative language of co-operative shaping, of common contribution, which the traditional concept of 'culture' so notably expressed, will be found preferable. In this fundamental choice there is no alternative, from any socialist position, to recognition and emphasis of the massive historical and immediate experience of class domination and subordination, in all their different forms. This becomes, very quickly, a matter of specific experience and argument. But there is a closely related problem within the concept of 'hegemony' itself. In some uses, though not I think in Gramsci, the totalizing tendency of the concept, which is significant and indeed crucial, is converted into an abstract totalization, and in this form it is readily compatible with sophisticated senses of 'the super-structure' or even 'ideology'. The hegemony, that is, can be seen as more uniform, more static, and more abstract than in practice, if it is really understood, it can ever actually be. Like any other Marxist concept it is particularly susceptible to epochal as distinct from historical definition, and to categorical as distinct from substantial description. Any isolation of its 'organizing principles', or of its 'determining features', which have indeed to be grasped in experience and by analysis, can lead very quickly to a totalizing abstraction. And then the problems of the reality of domination and subordination, and of their relations to co-operative shaping and common contribution, can be quite falsely posed.

A lived hegemony is always a process. It is not, except analytically, a system or a structure. It is a realized complex of experiences, relationships, and activities, with specific and changing pressures and limits. In practice, that is, hegemony can never be singular. Its internal structures are highly complex, as can readily be seen in any concrete analysis. Moreover (and this is crucial, reminding us of the necessary thrust of the concept), it does not just passively exist as a form of dominance. It has continually to be renewed, recreated, defended, and modified. It is also continually resisted, limited, altered, challenged by pressures not at all its own. We have then to add to the concept of hegemony the concepts of counter-hegemony and alternative hegemony, which are real and persistent elements of practice.

One way of expressing the necessary distinction between practical and abstract senses within the concept is to speak of 'the hegemonic' rather than the 'hegemony', and of 'the dominant' rather than simple 'domination'. The reality of any hegemony, in the extended political and cultural sense, is that, while by definition it is always dominant, it is never either total or exclusive. At any time, forms of alternative or directly oppositional politics and culture exist as significant elements in the society. We shall need to explore their conditions and their limits, but their active presence is decisive, not only because they have to be included in any historical (as distinct from epochal) analysis, but as forms which have had significant effect on the hegemonic process itself. That is to say, alternative political and cultural emphases, and the many forms of opposition and struggle, are important not only in themselves but as indicative features of what the hegemonic process has in practice had to work to control. A static hegemony, of the kind which is indicated by abstract totalizing definitions of a dominant 'ideology' or 'world-view', can ignore or isolate such alternatives and opposition, but to the extent that they are significant the decisive hegemonic function is to control or transform or even incorporate them. In this active process the hegemonic has to be seen as more than the simple transmission of an (unchanging) dominance. On the contrary, any hegemonic process must be especially alert and responsive to the alternatives and opposition which question or threaten its dominance. The reality of cultural process must then always include the efforts and contributions of those who are in one way or another outside or at the edge of the terms of the specific hegemony.

Thus it is misleading, as a general method, to reduce all political and cultural initiatives and contributions to the terms of the hegemony. That is the reductive consequence of the radically different concept of 'superstructure'. The specific functions of 'the hegemonic', 'the dominant', have always to be stressed, but not in ways which suggest any *a priori* totality. The most interesting and difficult part of any cultural analysis, in complex societies, is that which seeks to grasp the hegemonic in its active and formative but also its transformational processes.

Works of art, by their substantial and general character, are often especially important as sources of this complex evidence.

The major theoretical problem, with immediate effect on methods of analysis, is to distinguish between alternative and oppositional initiatives and contributions which are made within or against a specific hegemony (which then sets certain limits to them or which can succeed in neutralizing, changing or actually incorporating them) and other kinds of initiative and contribution which are irreducible to the terms of the original or the adaptive hegemony, and are in that sense independent. It can be persuasively argued that all or nearly all initiatives and contributions, even when they take on manifestly alternative or oppositional forms, are in practice tied to the hegemonic: that the dominant culture, so to say, at once produces and limits its own forms of counter-culture. There is more evidence for this view (for example in the case of the Romantic critique of industrial civilization) than we usually admit. But there is evident variation in specific kinds of social order and in the character of the consequent alternative and oppositional formations. It would be wrong to overlook the importance of works and ideas which, while clearly affected by hegemonic limits and pressures, are at least in part significant breaks beyond them, which may again in part be neutralized, reduced, or incorporated, but which in their most active elements nevertheless come through as independent and original.

Thus cultural process must not be assumed to be merely adaptive, extensive, and incorporative. Authentic breaks within and beyond it, in specific social conditions which can vary from extreme isolation to pre-revolutionary breakdowns and actual revolutionary activity, have often in fact occurred. And we are better able to see this, alongside more general recognition of the insistent pressures and limits of the hegemonic, if we develop modes of analysis which instead of reducing works to finished products, and activities to fixed positions, are capable of discerning, in good faith, the finite but significant openness of many actual initiatives and contributions. The finite but significant openness of many works of art, as signifying forms making possible but also requiring persistent and variable signifying responses, is then especially relevant.

7. Traditions, Institutions, and Formations

Hegemony is always an active process, but this does not mean that it is simply a complex of dominant features and elements. On the contrary, it is always a more or less adequate organization and interconnection of otherwise separated and even disparate meanings, values, and practices, which it specifically incorporates in a significant culture and an effective social order. These are themselves living resolutions—in the broadest sense, political resolutions—of specific economic realities. This process of incorporation is of major cultural importance. To understand it, but also to understand the material on which it must work, we need to distinguish three aspects of any cultural process, which we can call traditions, institutions, and formations.

The concept of tradition has been radically neglected in Marxist cultural thought. It is usually seen as at best a secondary factor, which may at most modify other and more decisive historical processes. This is not only because it is ordinarily diagnosed as superstructure, but also because 'tradition' has been commonly understood as a relatively inert, historicized segment of a social structure: tradition as the surviving past. But this version of tradition is weak at the very point where the incorporating sense of tradition is strong: where it is seen, in fact, as an actively shaping force. For tradition is in practice the most evident expression of the dominant and hegemonic pressures and limits. It is always more than an inert historicized segment; indeed it is the most powerful practical means of incorporation. What we have to see is not just 'a tradition' but a *selective tradition*: an intentionally selective version of a shaping past and a pre-shaped present, which is then powerfully operative in the process of social and cultural definition and identification.

It is usually not difficult to show this empirically. Most versions of 'tradition' can be quickly shown to be radically selective. From a whole possible area of past and present, in a particular culture, certain meanings and practices are selected for emphasis and certain other meanings and practices are neglected or excluded. Yet, within a particular hegemony, and as one of its decisive processes, this selection is presented and usually successfully passed off as 'the tradition', 'the significant past'. What has then to be said about any tradition is that it is in this sense an aspect of *contemporary* social and cultural organization, in the interest of the dominance of a specific class. It is a version of the past which is intended to connect with and ratify the present. What it offers in practice is a sense of *predisposed continuity*.

There are, it is true, weaker senses of 'tradition', in explicit contrast to 'innovation' and 'the contemporary'. These are often points of retreat for groups in the society which have been left stranded by some particular hegemonic development. All that is now left to them is the retrospective affirmation of 'traditional values'. Or, from an opposite position, 'traditional habits' are isolated, by some current hegemonic development, as elements of the past which have now to be discarded. Much of the overt argument about tradition is conducted between representatives of these two positions. But at a deeper level the hegemonic sense of tradition is always the most active: a deliberately selective and connecting process which offers a historical and cultural ratification of a contemporary order.

It is a very powerful process, since it is tied to many practical continuities—families, places, institutions, a language—which are indeed directly experienced. It is also, at any time, a vulnerable process, since it has in practice to discard whole areas of significance, or reinterpret or dilute them, or convert them into forms which support or at least do not contradict the really important elements of the current hegemony. It is significant that much of the most accessible and influential work of the counter-hegemony is historical: the recovery of discarded areas, or the redress of selective and reductive interpretations. But this in turn has little effect unless the lines to the present, in the actual process of the selective tradition, are clearly and actively traced. Otherwise any recovery can be simply residual or marginal. It is at the vital points of *connection*, where a version of the past is used to ratify the present and to indicate directions for the future, that a selective tradition is at once powerful and vulnerable. Powerful because it is so skilled in making active selective connections, dismissing those it does not want as 'out of date' or 'nostalgic', attacking those it cannot incorporate as 'unprecedented' or 'alien.' Vulnerable because the real record is effectively recoverable, and many of the alternative or opposing practical continuities are still available. Vulnerable also because the selective version of 'a living tradition' is always tied, though often in complex and hidden ways, to explicit contemporary pressures and limits. Its practical inclusions and exclusions are selectively encouraged or discouraged, often so effectively that the deliberate selection is made to verify itself in practice. Yet its selective privileges and interests, material in substance but often ideal in form, including complex elements of style and tone and of basic method, can still be recognized, demonstrated, and broken. This struggle for and against selective traditions is understandably a major part of all contemporary cultural activity.

It is true that the effective establishment of a selective tradition can be said to depend on identifiable institutions. But it is an underestimate of the process to suppose that it depends on institutions alone. The relations between cultural, political, and economic institutions are themselves very complex, and the substance of these relations is a direct indication of the character of the culture in the wider sense. But it is never only a question of formally identifiable institutions. It is also a question of *formations*; those effective movements and tendencies, in intellectual and artistic life, which have significant and sometimes decisive influence on the active development of a culture, and which have a variable and often oblique relation to formal institutions.

Formal institutions, evidently, have a profound influence on the active social process. What is abstracted in orthodox sociology as 'socialization' is in practice, in any actual society, a specific kind of incorporation. Its description as 'socialization', the universal abstract process on which all human beings can be said to depend, is a way of avoiding or hiding this specific content and intention. Any process of socialization of course includes things that all human beings have to learn, but any specific process ties this necessary learning to a selected range of meanings, values, and practices which, in the very closeness of their association with necessary learning, constitute the real foundations of the hegemonic. In a family children are cared for and taught to care for themselves, but within this necessary process fundamental and selective attitudes to self, to others, to a social order, and to the material world are both consciously and unconsciously taught. Education transmits necessary knowledge and skills, but always by a particular selection from the whole available range, and with intrinsic attitudes, both to learning and social relations, which are in practice virtually inextricable. Institutions such as churches are explicitly incorporative. Specific communities and specific places of work, exerting powerful and immediate pressures on the conditions of living and of making a living, teach, confirm, and in most cases finally enforce selected meanings, values, and activities. To describe the effect of all institutions of these kinds is to arrive at an important but still incomplete understanding of incorporation. In modern societies we have to add the major communications systems. These materialize selected news and opinion, and a wide range of selected perceptions and attitudes.

Yet it can still not be supposed that the sum of all these institutions is an organic hegemony. On the contrary, just because it is not 'socialization' but a specific and complex hegemonic process, it is in practice full of contradictions and of unresolved conflicts. This is why it must not be reduced to the activities of an 'ideological state apparatus'. Such apparatus exists, although variably, but the whole process is much wider, and is in some important respects self-generating. By selection it is possible to identify common features in family, school, community, work, and communications, and these are important. But just because they are specific processes, with variable particular purposes, and with variable but always effective relations with what must in any case, in the short term, be done, the practical consequence is as often confusion and conflict between what are experienced as different purposes and different values, as it is crude incorporation of a theoretical kind. An effective incorporation is usually in practice achieved; indeed to establish and maintain a class society it must be achieved. But no mere training or pressure is truly hegemonic. The true condition of hegemony is effective *self-identification* with the hegemonic forms: a specific and internalized 'socialization' which is expected to be positive but which, if that is not possible, will rest on a (resigned) recognition of the inevitable and the necessary. An effective culture, in this sense, is always more than the sum of its institutions: not only because these can be seen, in analysis, to derive much of their character from it, but mainly because it is at the level of a whole culture that the crucial *interrelations*, including confusions and conflicts, are really negotiated.

This is why, in any analysis, we have also to include *forma-*

tions. These are most recognizable as conscious movements and tendencies (literary, artistic, philosophical or scientific) which can usually be readily discerned after their formative productions. Often, when we look further, we find that these are articulations of much wider effective formations. which can by no means be wholly identified with formal institutions, or their formal meanings and values, and which can sometimes even be positively contrasted with them. This factor is of the greatest importance for the understanding of what is habitually specialized as intellectual and artistic life. In this fundamental relation between the institutions and formations of a culture there is great historical variability, but it is generally characteristic of developed complex societies that formations, as distinct from institutions, play an increasingly important role. Moreover, since such formations relate, inevitably, to real social structures, and yet have highly variable and often oblique relations with formally discernible social institutions, any social and cultural analysis of them requires procedures radically different from those developed for institutions. What is really being analysed, in each case, is a mode of specialized practice. Moreover, within an apparent hegemony, which can be readily described in generalizing ways, there are not only alternative and oppositional formations (some of them, at certain historical stages, having become or in the process of becoming alternative and oppositional institutions) but, within what can be recognized as the dominant, effectively varying formations which resist any simple reduction to some generalized hegemonic function.

It is at this point, normally, that many of those in real contact with such formations and their work retreat to an indifferent emphasis on the complexity of cultural activity. Others altogether deny (even theoretically) the relation of such formations and such work to the social process and especially the material social process. Others again, when the historical reality of the formations is grasped, render this back to ideal constructions—national traditions, literary and artistic traditions, histories of ideas, psychological types, spiritual archetypes—which indeed acknowledge and define formations, often much more substantially than the usual generalizing accounts of explicit social derivation or superstructural function, but only by radically displacing them from the immediate cultural process.

As a result of this displacement, the formations and their work are not seen as the active social and cultural substance that they quite invariably are. In our own culture, this form of displacement, made temporarily or comparatively convincing by the failures of derivative and superstructural interpretation, is itself, and quite centrally, hegemonic.

8. Dominant, Residual, and Emergent

The complexity of a culture is to be found not only in its variable processes and their social definitions—traditions, institutions, and formations—but also in the dynamic interrelations, at every point in the process, of historically varied and variable elements. In what I have called 'epochal' analysis, a cultural process is seized as a cultural system, with determinate dominant features: feudal culture or bourgeois culture or a transition from one to the other. This emphasis on dominant and definitive lineaments and features is important and often, in practice, effective. But it then often happens that its methodology is preserved for the very different function of historical analysis, in which a sense of movement within what is ordinarily abstracted as a system is crucially necessary, especially if it is to connect with the future as well as with the past. In authentic historical analysis it is necessary at every point to recognize the complex interrelations between movements and tendencies both within and beyond a specific and effective dominance. It is necessary to examine how these relate to the whole cultural process rather than only to the selected and abstracted dominant system. Thus 'bourgeois culture' is a significant generalizing description and hypothesis, expressed within epochal analysis by fundamental comparisons with 'feudal culture' or 'socialist culture'. However, as a description of cultural process, over four or five centuries and in scores of different societies, it requires immediate historical and internally comparative differentiation. Moreover, even if this is acknowledged or practically carried out, the 'epochal' definition can exert its pressure as a static type against which all real cultural process is measured, either to show 'stages' or 'variations' of the type (which is still historical analysis) or, at its worst, to select supporting and exclude 'marginal' or 'incidental' or 'secondary' evidence.

Such errors are avoidable if, while retaining the epochal hypothesis, we can find terms which recognize not only 'stages' and 'variations' but the internal dynamic relations of any actual process. We have certainly still to speak of the 'dominant' and the 'effective', and in these senses of the hegemonic. But we find that we have also to speak, and indeed with further differentiation of each, of the 'residual' and the 'emergent', which in any real process, and at any moment in the process, are significant both in themselves and in what they reveal of the characteristics of the 'dominant'.

By 'residual' I mean something different from the 'archaic', though in practice these are often very difficult to distinguish. Any culture includes available elements of its past, but their place in the contemporary cultural process is profoundly variable. I would call the 'archaic' that which is wholly recognized as an element of the past, to be observed, to be examined, or even on occasion to be consciously 'revived', in a deliberately specializing way. What I mean by the 'residual' is very different. The residual, by definition, has been effectively formed in the past, but it is still active in the cultural process, not only and often not at all as an element of the past, but as an effective element of the present. Thus certain experiences, meanings, and values which cannot be expressed or substantially verified in terms of the dominant culture, are nevertheless lived and practised on the basis of the residue—cultural as well as social—of some previous social and cultural institution or formation. It is crucial to distinguish this aspect of the residual, which may have an alternative or even oppositional relation to the dominant culture, from that active manifestation of the residual (this being its distinction from the archaic) which has been wholly or largely incorporated into the dominant culture. In three characteristic cases in contemporary English culture this distinction can become a precise term of analysis. Thus organized religion is predominantly residual, but within this there is a significant difference between some practically alternative and oppositional meanings and values (absolute brotherhood, service to others without reward) and a larger body of incorporated meanings and values (official morality, or the social order of which the other-worldly is a separated neutralizing or ratifying component). Again, the idea of rural community is predominantly residual, but is in some limited respects alternative or oppositional to urban industrial capitalism, though for the most part it is incorporated, as idealization or fantasy, or as an exotic—residential or escape—leisure function of the dominant order itself. Again, in monarchy, there is virtually nothing that is actively residual (alternative or oppositional), but, with a heavy and deliberate additional use of the archaic, a residual function has been wholly incorporated as a specific political and cultural function—marking the limits as well as the methods—of a form of capitalist democracy.

A residual cultural element is usually at some distance from the effective dominant culture, but some part of it, some version of it —and especially if the residue is from some major area of the past—will in most cases have had to be incorporated if the effective dominant culture is to make sense in these areas. Moreover, at certain points the dominant culture cannot allow too much residual experience and practice outside itself, at least without risk. It is in the incorporation of the actively residual —by reinterpretation, dilution, projection, discriminating inclusion and exclusion—that the work of the selective tradition is especially evident. This is very notable in the case of versions of 'the literary tradition', passing through selective versions of the character of literature to connecting and incorporated definitions of what literature now is and should be. This is one among several crucial areas, since it is in some alternative or even oppositional versions of what literature is (has been) and what literary experience (and in one common derivation, other significant experience) is and must be, that, against the pressures of incorporation, actively residual meanings and values are sustained.

By 'emergent' I mean, first, that new meanings and values, new practices, new relationships and kinds of relationship are continually being created. But it is exceptionally difficult to distinguish between those which are really elements of some new phase of the dominant culture (and in this sense 'species-specific') and those which are substantially alternative or oppositional to it: emergent in the strict sense, rather than merely novel. Since we are always considering relations within a cultural process, definitions of the emergent, as of the residual, can be made only in relation to a full sense of the dominant. Yet the social location of the residual is always easier to understand, since a large part of it (though not all) relates to earlier social formations and phases of the cultural process, in which certain real meanings and values were generated. In the subsequent default of a particular phase of a dominant culture there is then a reaching back to those meanings and values which were created in actual societies and actual situations in the past, and which still seem to have significance because they represent areas of human experience, aspiration, and achievement which the dominant culture neglects, undervalues, opposes, represses, or even cannot recognize.

The case of the emergent is radically different. It is true that in the structure of any actual society, and especially in its class structure, there is always a social basis for elements of the cultural process that are alternative or oppositional to the dominant elements. One kind of basis has been valuably described in the central body of Marxist theory: the formation of a new class, the coming to consciousness of a new class, and within this, in actual process, the (often uneven) emergence of elements of a new cultural formation. Thus the emergence of the working class as a class was immediately evident (for example, in nineteenth-century England) in the cultural process. But there was extreme unevenness of contribution in different parts of the process. The making of new social values and institutions far outpaced the making of strictly cultural institutions, while specific cultural contributions, though significant, were less vigorous and autonomous than either general or institutional innovation. A new class is always a source of emergent cultural practice, but while it is still, as a class, relatively subordinate, this is always likely to be uneven and is certain to be incomplete. For new practice is not, of course, an isolated process. To the degree that it emerges, and especially to the degree that it is oppositional rather than alternative, the process of attempted incorporation significantly begins. This can be seen, in the same period in England, in the emergence and then the effective incorporation of a radical popular press. It can be seen in the emergence and incorporation of working-class writing, where the fundamental problem of emergence is clearly revealed, since the basis of incorporation, in such cases, is the effective predominance of received literary forms—an incorporation, so to say, which already conditions and limits the emergence. But the development is always uneven. Straight incorporation is most directly attempted against the visibly alternative and oppositional class elements: trade unions, working-class political parties, working-class life styles (as incorporated into 'popular' journalism, advertising, and commercial entertainment). The process of emergence, in such conditions, is then a constantly repeated, an always renewable, move beyond a phase of practical incorporation: usually made much more difficult by the fact that much incorporation looks like recognition, acknowledgement, and thus a form of *acceptance*. In this complex process there is indeed regular confusion between the locally residual (as a form of resistance to incorporation) and the generally emergent.

Cultural emergence in relation to the emergence and growing strength of a class is then always of major importance, and always complex. But we have also to see that it is not the only kind of emergence. This recognition is very difficult, theoretically, though the practical evidence is abundant. What has really to be said, as a way of defining important elements of both the residual and the emergent, and as a way of understanding the character of the dominant, is that *no mode of production and therefore no dominant social order and therefore no dominant culture ever in reality includes or exhausts all human practice, human energy, and human intention*. This is not merely a negative proposition, allowing us to account for significant things which happen outside or against the dominant mode. On the contrary it is a fact about the modes of domination, that they select from and consequently exclude the full range of human practice. What they exclude may often be seen as the personal or the private, or as the natural or even the metaphysical. Indeed it is usually in one or other of these terms that the excluded area is expressed, since what the dominant has effectively seized is indeed the ruling definition of the social.

It is this seizure that has especially to be resisted. For there is always, though in varying degrees, practical consciousness, in specific relationships, specific skills, specific perceptions, that is unquestionably social and that a specifically dominant social order neglects, excludes, represses, or simply fails to recognize. A distinctive and comparative feature of any dominant social order is how far it reaches into the whole range of practices and experiences in an attempt at incorporation. There can be areas of experience it is willing to ignore or dispense with: to assign as private or to specialize as aesthetic or to generalize as natural. Moreover, as a social order changes, in terms of its own developing needs, these relations are variable. Thus in advanced capitalism, because of changes in the social character of labour, in the social character of communications, and in the social character of decision-making, the dominant culture reaches much further than ever before in capitalist society into hitherto 'reserved' or 'resigned' areas of experience and practice and meaning. The area of effective penetration of the dominant order into the whole social and cultural process is thus now significantly greater. This in turn makes the problem of emergence especially acute, and narrows the gap between alternative and oppositional elements. The alternative, especially in areas that impinge on significant areas of the dominant, is often seen as oppositional and, by pressure, often converted into it. Yet even here there can be spheres of practice and meaning which, almost by definition from its own limited character, or in its profound deformation, the dominant culture is unable in any real terms to recognize. Elements of emergence may indeed be incorporated, but just as often the incorporated forms are merely facsimiles of the genuinely emergent cultural practice. Any significant emergence, beyond or against a dominant mode, is very difficult under these conditions; in itself and in its repeated confusion with the facsimiles and novelties of the incorporated phase. Yet, in our own period as in others, the fact of emergent cultural practice is still undeniable, and together with the fact of actively residual practice is a necessary complication of the would-be dominant culture.

This complex process can still in part be described in class terms. But there is always other social being and consciousness which is neglected and excluded: alternative perceptions of others, in immediate relationships; new perceptions and practices of the material world. In practice these are different in quality from the developing and articulated interests of a rising class. The relations between these two sources of the emergent—the class and the excluded social (human) area—are by no means necessarily contradictory. At times they can be very close and on the relations between them much in political practice depends. But culturally and as a matter of theory the areas can be seen as distinct.

What matters, finally, in understanding emergent culture, as distinct from both the dominant and the residual, is that it is never only a matter of immediate practice; indeed it depends crucially on finding new forms or adaptations of form. Again and again what we have to observe is in effect a *pre-emergence*, active and pressing but not yet fully articulated, rather than the evident emergence which could be more confidently named. It is to understand more closely this condition of pre-emergence, as well as the more evident forms of the emergent, the residual, and the dominant, that we need to explore the concept of structures of feeling.

9. Structures of Feeling

In most description and analysis, culture and society are expressed in an habitual past tense. The strongest barrier to the recognition of human cultural activity is this immediate and regular conversion of experience into finished products. What is defensible as a procedure in conscious history, where on certain assumptions many actions can be definitively taken as having ended, is habitually projected, not only into the always moving substance of the past, but into contemporary life, in which relationships, institutions and formations in which we are still actively involved are converted, by this procedural mode, into formed wholes rather than forming and formative processes. Analysis is then centred on relations between these produced institutions, formations, and experiences, so that now, as in that produced past, only the fixed explicit forms exist, and living presence is always, by definition, receding.

When we begin to grasp the dominance of this procedure, to look into its centre and if possible past its edges, we can understand, in new ways, that separation of the social from the personal which is so powerful and directive a cultural mode. If the social is always past, in the sense that it is always formed, we have indeed to find other terms for the undeniable experience of the present: not only the temporal present, the realization of this and this instant, but the specificity of present being, the inalienably physical, within which we may indeed discern and acknowledge institutions, formations, positions, but not always as fixed products, defining products. And then if the social is the fixed and explicit—the known relationships, institutions, formations, positions—all that is present and moving, all that escapes or seems to escape from the fixed and the explicit and the known, is grasped and defined as the personal: this, here, now, alive, active, 'subjective'.

There is another related distinction. As thought is described, in the same habitual past tense, it is indeed so different, in its explicit and finished forms, from much or even anything that we can presently recognize as thinking, that we set against it more active, more flexible, less singular terms—consciousness, experience, feeling—and then watch even these drawn towards fixed, finite, receding forms. The point is especially relevant to works of art, which really are, in one sense, explicit and finished forms—actual objects in the visual arts, objectified conventions and notations (semantic figures) in literature. But it is not only that, to complete their inherent process, we have to make them present, in specifically active 'readings'. It is also that the making of art is never itself in the past tense. It is always a formative process, within a specific present. At different moments in history, and in significantly different ways, the reality and even the primacy of such presences and such processes, such diverse and yet specific actualities, have been powerfully asserted and reclaimed, as in practice of course they are all the time lived. But they are then often asserted as forms themselves, in contention with other known forms: the subjective as distinct from the objective; experience from belief; feeling from thought; the immediate from the general; the personal from the social. The undeniable power of two great modern ideological systems—the 'aesthetic' and the 'psychological'—is, ironically, systematically derived from these senses of instance and process, where experience, immediate feeling, and then subjectivity and personality are newly generalized and assembled. Against these 'personal' forms, the ideological systems of fixed social generality, of categorical products, of absolute formations, are relatively powerless, within their specific dimension. Of one dominant strain in Marxism, with its habitual abuse of the 'subjective' and the 'personal', this is especially true.

Yet it is the reduction of the social to fixed forms that remains the basic error. Marx often said this, and some Marxists quote him, in fixed ways, before returning to fixed forms. The mistake, as so often, is in taking terms of analysis as terms of substance. Thus we speak of a world-view or of a prevailing ideology or of a class outlook, often with adequate evidence, but in this regular slide towards a past tense and a fixed form suppose, or even do not know that we have to suppose, that these exist and are lived specifically and definitively, in singular and developing forms. Perhaps the dead can be reduced to fixed forms, though their surviving records are against it. But the living will not be reduced, at least in the first person; living third persons may be different. All the known complexities, the experienced tensions, shifts, and uncertainties, the intricate forms of unevenness and confusion, are against the terms of the reduction and soon, by extension, against social analysis itself. Social forms are then often admitted for generalities but debarred, contemptuously, from any possible relevance to this immediate and actual significance of being. And from the abstractions formed in their turn by this act of debarring—the 'human imagination', the 'human psyche', the 'unconscious', with their 'functions' in art and in myth and in dream—new and displaced forms of social analysis and categorization, overriding all specific social conditions, are then more or less rapidly developed.

Social forms are evidently more recognizable when they are articulate and explicit. We have seen this in the range from institutions to formations and traditions. We can see it again in the range from dominant systems of belief and education to influential systems of explanation and argument. All these have effective presence. Many are formed and deliberate, and some are quite fixed. But when they have all been identified they are not a whole inventory even of social consciousness in its simplest sense. For they become social consciousness only when they are lived, actively, in real relationships, and moreover in relationships which are more than systematic exchanges between fixed units. Indeed just because all consciousness is social, its processes occur not only between but within the relationship and the related. And this practical consciousness is always more than a handling of fixed forms and units. There is frequent tension between the received interpretation and practical experience. Where this tension can be made direct and explicit, or where some alternative interpretation is available, we are still within a dimension of relatively fixed forms. But the tension is as often an unease, a stress, a displacement, a latency: the moment of conscious comparison not yet come, often not even coming. And comparison is by no means the only process, though it is powerful and important. There are the experiences to which the fixed forms do not speak at all, which indeed they do not recognize. There are important mixed experiences, where the available meaning would convert part to all, or all to part. And even where form and response can be found to agree, without apparent difficulty, there can be qualifications, reservations, indications elsewhere: what the agreement seemed to settle but still sounding elsewhere. Practical consciousness is almost always different from official consciousness, and this is not only a matter of relative freedom or control. For practical consciousness is what is actually being lived, and not only what it is thought is being lived. Yet the actual alternative to the received and produced fixed forms is not silence: not the absence, the unconscious, which bourgeois culture has mythicized. It is a kind of feeling and thinking which is indeed social and material, but each in an embryonic phase before it can become fully articulate and defined exchange. Its relations with the already articulate and defined are then exceptionally complex.

This process can be directly observed in the history of a language. In spite of substantial and at some levels decisive continuities in grammar and vocabulary, no generation speaks quite the same language as its predecessors. The difference can be defined in terms of additions, deletions, and modifications, but these do not exhaust it. What really changes is something quite general, over a wide range, and the description that often fits the change best is the literary term 'style'. It is a general change, rather than a set of deliberate choices, yet choices can be deduced from it, as well as effects. Similar kinds of change can be observed in manners, dress, building, and other similar forms of social life. It is an open question—that is to say, a set of specific historical questions—whether in any of these changes this or that group has been dominant or influential, or whether they are the result of much more general interaction. For what we are defining is a particular quality of social experience and relationship, historically distinct from other particular qualities, which gives the sense of a generation or of a period. The relations between this quality and the other specifying historical marks of changing institutions, formations, and beliefs, and beyond these the changing social and economic relations between and within classes, are again an open question: that is to say, a set of specific historical questions. The methodological consequence of such a definition, however, is that the specific qualitative changes are not *assumed* to be epiphenomena of changed institutions, formations, and beliefs, or merely secondary evidence of changed social and economic relations between and within classes. At the same time they are from the beginning taken as *social* experience, rather than as 'personal' experience or as the merely superficial or incidental 'small change' of society. They are social in two ways that distinguish them from reduced senses of the social as the institutional and the formal: first, in that they are *changes of* presence (while they are being lived this is obvious; when they have been lived it is still their substantial characteristic); second, in that although they are emergent or pre-emergent, they do not have to await definition, classification, or rationalization before they exert palpable pressures and set effective limits on experience and on action.

Such changes can be defined as changes in *structures of feeling*. The term is difficult, but 'feeling' is chosen to emphasize a distinction from more formal concepts of 'world-view' or 'ideology'. It is not only that we must go beyond formally held and systematic beliefs, though of course we have always to include them. It is that we are concerned with meanings and values as they are actively lived and felt, and the relations between these and formal or systematic beliefs are in practice variable (including historically variable), over a range from formal assent with private dissent to the more nuanced interaction between selected and interpreted beliefs and acted and justified experiences. An alternative definition would be structures of experience: in one sense the better and wider word, but with the difficulty that one of its senses has that past tense which is the most important obstacle to recognition of the area of social experience which is being defined. We are talking about characteristic elements of impulse, restraint, and tone; specifically affective elements of consciousness and relationships: not feeling against thought, but thought as felt and feeling as thought: practical consciousness of a present kind, in a living and interrelating continuity. We are then defining these elements as a 'structure': as a set, with specific internal relations, at once interlocking and in tension. Yet we are also defining a social experience which is still *in process*, often indeed not yet recognized as social but taken to be private, idiosyncratic, and even isolating, but which in analysis (though rarely otherwise) has its emergent, connecting, and dominant characteristics, indeed its specific hierarchies. These are often more recognizable at a later stage, when they have been (as often happens) formalized, classified, and in many cases built into institutions and formations. By that time the case is different; a new structure of feeling will usually already have begun to form, in the true social present.

Methodologically, then, a 'structure of feeling' is a cultural hypothesis, actually derived from attempts to understand such elements and their connections in a generation or period, and needing always to be returned, interactively, to such evidence. It is initially less simple than more formally structured hypotheses of the social, but it is more adequate to the actual range of cultural evidence: historically certainly, but even more (where it matters more) in our present cultural process. The hypothesis has a special relevance to art and literature, where the true social content is in a significant number of cases of this present and affective kind, which cannot without loss be reduced to belief-systems, institutions, or explicit general relationships, though it may include all these as lived and experienced, with or without tension, as it also evidently includes elements of social and material (physical or natural) experience which may lie beyond, or be uncovered or imperfectly covered by, the elsewhere recognizable systematic elements. The unmistakable presence of certain elements in art which are not covered by (though in one mode they may be reduced to) other formal systems is the true source of the specializing categories of 'the aesthetic', 'the arts', and 'imaginative literature'. We need, on the one hand, to acknowledge (and welcome) the specificity of these elements—specific feelings, specific rhythms—and yet to find ways of recognizing their specific kinds of sociality, thus preventing that extraction from social experience which is conceivable only when social experience itself has been categorically (and at root historically) reduced. We are then not only concerned with the restoration of social content in its full sense, that of a generative immediacy. The idea of a structure of feeling can be specifically related to the evidence of forms and conventions—semantic figures—which, in art and literature, are often among the very first indications that such a new structure is forming. These relations will be discussed in more detail in subsequent chapters, but as a matter of cultural theory this is a way of defining forms and conventions in art and literature as inalienable elements of a social material process: not by derivation from other social forms and pre-forms, but as social formation of a specific kind which may in turn be seen as the articulation (often the only fully available articulation) of structures of feeling which as living processes are much more widely experienced.

For structures of feeling can be defined as social experiences *in solution*, as distinct from other social semantic formations which have been *precipitated* and are more evidently and more immediately available. Not all art, by any means, relates to a contemporary structure of feeling. The effective formations of most actual art relate to already manifest social formations, dominant or residual, and it is primarily to emergent formations (though often in the form of modification or disturbance in older forms) that the structure of feeling, *as solution*, relates. Yet this specific solution is never mere flux. It is a structured formation which, because it is at the very edge of semantic availability, has many of the characteristics of a pre-formation, until specific articulations—new semantic figures—are discovered in material practice: often, as it happens, in relatively isolated ways, which are only later seen to compose a significant (often in fact minority) generation; this often, in turn, the generation that substantially connects to its successors. It is thus a specific structure of particular linkages, particular emphases and suppressions, and, in what are often its most recognizable forms, particular deep starting-points and conclusions. Early Victorian ideology, for example, specified the exposure caused by poverty or by debt or by illegitimacy as social failure or deviation; the contemporary structure of feeling, meanwhile, in the new semantic figures of Dickens, of Emily Brontë, and others, specified exposure and isolation as a *general* condition, and poverty, debt, or illegitimacy as its connecting instances. An alternative ideology, relating such exposure to the nature of the social order, was only later generally formed: offering explanations but now at a reduced tension: the social explanation fully admitted, the intensity of experienced fear and shame now dispersed and generalized.

The example reminds us, finally, of the complex relation of differentiated structures of feeling to differentiated classes. This is historically very variable. In England between 1660 and 1690, for example, two structures of feeling (among the defeated Puritans and in the restored Court) can be readily distinguished, though neither, in its literature and elsewhere, is reducible to the ideologies of these groups or to their formal (in fact complex) class relations. At times the emergence of a new structure of feeling is best related to the rise of a class (England, 1700-60); at other times to contradiction, fracture, or mutation within a class (England, 1780–1830 or 1890–1930), when a formation appears to break away from its class norms, though it retains its substantial affiliation, and the tension is at once lived and articulated in radically new semantic figures. Any of these examples requires detailed substantiation, but what is now in question, theoretically, is the hypothesis of a mode of social formation, explicit and recognizable in specific kinds of art, which is distinguishable from other social and semantic formations by its articulation of presence.

10. The Sociology of Culture

Many of the procedures of sociology have been limited or distorted by reduced and reductive concepts of society and the social. This is particularly evident in the sociology of culture. Within the radical empiricist tradition, often practically associated with Marxism, there has been important work on institutions. The major modern communications systems are now so evidently key institutions in advanced capitalist societies that they require the same kind of attention, at least initially, that is given to the institutions of industrial production and distribution. Studies of the ownership and control of the capitalist press, the capitalist cinema, and capitalist and state-capitalist radio and television interlock, historically and theoretically, with wider analyses of capitalist society, capitalist economy, and the neo-capitalist state. Further, many of the same institutions require analysis in the context of modern imperialism and neo-colonialism, to which they are crucially relevant (see Schiller (1969)).

Over and above their empirical results, these analyses force theoretical revision of the formula of base and superstructure and of the definition of productive forces, in a social area in which large-scale capitalist economic activity and cultural production are now inseparable. Unless this theoretical revision is made, even the best work of the radical and anti-capitalist empiricists is in the end overlaid or absorbed by the specific theoretical structures of bourgeois cultural sociology. The bourgeois concept of 'mass communications' and the tied radical concept of 'mass manipulation' are alike inadequate to the true sociology of these central and varying institutions. Even at an early stage of analysis these undifferentiated and blocking concepts need to be replaced by the motivating and specifying terms of hegemony. What both bourgeois and radical-empiricist cultural theory have achieved is the social *neutralization* of such institutions: the concept of the 'mass' replacing and neutralizing specific class structures; the concept of 'manipulation' (an operative strategy in capitalist advertising and politics) replacing and neutralizing the complex interactions of control, selection, incorporation, and the phases of social consciousness which correspond to real social situations and relations.

This neutralizing element has been particularly evident in the study of 'effects' which has preoccupied empirical bourgeois sociology. Here the analysis and even the recognition of 'effects' are predetermined by the assumption of norms which are either, like 'socialization', abstract and mystifying (since it is precisely the historical and class variations of 'socialization' which need to be studied) or, as in the studies of effects on politics or on 'violence', are themselves 'effects' of a whole active social order, which is not analysed but simply taken as background or as an empirical 'control'. The complex sociology of actual audiences, and of the real conditions of reception and response in these highly variable systems (the cinema audience, the newspaper readership, and the television audience being highly distinct social structures), is overlaid by bourgeois norms of 'cultural producers' and 'the mass public', with the additional effect that the complex sociology of these producers, as managers and agents within capitalist systems, is itself not developed.

A further effect of this kind of concentration on 'mass communications' is that analysis is not normally extended to institutions where these norms appear to be absent: for example, book publishing, which is now undergoing a critical phase of capitalist reorganization with cultural effects which are often not seen as a problem because they are not a 'mass' problem. There has been frequent and often justified complaint against 'vulgar Marxism', but the increasing penetration of small-scale capitalist institutions—which had carried the liberal ideology of 'true' cultural production (as distinct from 'mass culture')—by large-scale international investment and integration with many other forms of production is at once an economic and a cultural fact.

Cultural effects need not always be indirect. It is in practice impossible to separate the development of the novel as a literary form from the highly specific economics of fiction publication. This has been true, with many negative effects, (often isolated and projected as simple changes of sensibility or technique) since at latest the 1890s, though directly negative effects are now much more evident. Analysis of the sociology of the novel has to include many factors, but always this directly economic factor which, for ideological reasons, is ordinarily excluded. The insertion of economic determinations into cultural studies is of course the special contribution of Marxism, and there are times when its simple insertion is an evident advance. But in the end it can never be a simple insertion, since what is really required, beyond the limiting formulas, is restoration of the whole social material process, and specifically of cultural production as social and material. This is where analysis of institutions has to be extended to analysis of formations. The complex and variable sociology of those cultural formations which have no direct or exclusive or manifest institutional realization—literary and intellectual 'movements', for example—is especially important. Gramsci's work on intellectuals and Benjamin's work on 'bohemians' are encouraging models of an experimental Marxist kind.

A Marxist cultural sociology is then recognizable, in its simplest outlines, in studies of different types of institution and formation in cultural production and distribution, and in the linking of these within whole social material processes. Thus distribution, for example, is not limited to its technical definition and function within a capitalist market, but connected, specifically, to modes of production and then interpreted as the active formation of readerships and audiences, and of the characteristic social relations, including economic relations, within which particular forms of cultural activity are in practice carried out.

So much remains to be done, within this general outline, that it is tempting to rest on it. But we have seen, theoretically, as we learn again and again to see practically, that the reduction of social relations and social content to these explicit and manifest general forms is disabling. To these Marxist or other studies of institutions and formations it is crucially necessary to add studies of *forms*: not by way of illustration but, in many cases, as the most specific point of entry to certain kinds of formation. Here another and very different sociological tradition is relevant.

The sociology of consciousness, which was a seminal element in the period of classical sociology, and which led to a programmatic distinction of the 'cultural sciences', has remained influential and is well represented within the Marxist tradition by Lukács and Goldmann, and by the Frankfurt School. The general tendency, within bourgeois sociology, has been a reduction of the sociology of consciousness to the 'sociology of knowledge'. Within the empirical tradition there has been a further reduction to a sociology of the institutions of 'organized knowledge', such as education and religion, where a familiar kind of evidence, in consciously organized ideas and relationships, is more available. Within some Marxist tendencies, even, the understanding of 'consciousness' as 'knowledge'—perhaps primarily determined by positivism—has been especially weak in relation to important kinds of art and literature. For consciousness is not only knowledge, just as language is not only indication and naming. It is also what is elsewhere, and in this context necessarily, specialized as 'imagination'. In cultural production (and all consciousness is in this sense produced) the true range is from information and description, or naming and indication, to embodiment and *performance*. While the sociology of consciousness is limited to knowledge, all other real cultural processes are displaced from the social dimension in which, quite as evidently, they belong.

Thus a sociology of drama, already concerned with institutions (theatres and their predecessors and successors), with formations (groups of dramatists, dramatic and theatrical movements), with formed relationships (audiences, including the formation of audiences within theatres and their wider social formation), would go on to include forms, not only in the sense of their relations to world-views or structures of feeling but also in the more active sense of their whole performance (social methods of speaking, moving, representing, and so on). Indeed in many arts, while the manifest social content is evident in one way in institutions, formations, and communicative relationships, and in another way in forms which relate to specific selections of issues, specific kinds of interpretation and of course specifically reproduced content, an equally important and sometimes more fundamental social content can be found in the basic social means—historically variable and always active social forms of language and movement and representation—on which, ultimately, the more manifest social elements can be seen to depend.

Specific studies must often temporarily isolate this or that element. But the fundamental principle of a sociology of culture is the complex unity of the elements thus listed or separated. Indeed the most basic task of the sociology of culture is analysis of the interrelationships within this complex unity: a task distinct from the reduced sociology of institutions, formations, and communicative relationships and yet, as a sociology, radically distinct also from the analysis of isolated forms. As so often, the two dominant tendencies of bourgeois cultural studies—the sociology of the reduced but explicit 'society' and the aesthetics of the excluded social remade as a specialized 'art'—support and ratify each other in a significant division of labour. Everything can be known about a reading public, back to the economics of printing and publishing and the effects of an educational system, but what is read by that public is the neutralized abstraction 'books', or at best its catalogued categories. Meanwhile, but elsewhere, everything can be known about the books, back to their authors, to traditions and influences, and to periods, but these are finished objects before they go out into the dimension where 'sociology' is thought to be relevant: the reading public, the history of publishing. It is this division, now ratified by confident disciplines, which a sociology of culture has to overcome and supersede, insisting on what is always a whole and connected social material process. This is of course difficult, but great energy is now expended, and is often in effect trapped, in maintaining the abstract divisions and separations. Meanwhile in cultural practice and among cultural producers, before these received abstractions get to work, the process is inevitably known, if often indistinctly and unevenly, as whole and connected.

Specific methods of analysis will vary, in different areas of cultural activity. But one new method is now emerging, which can be felt as original in a number of fields. For if we have learned to see the relation of any cultural work to what we have learned to call a 'sign-system' (and this has been the important contribution of cultural semiotics), we can also come to see that a sign-system is itself a specific structure of social relationships: 'internally', in that the signs depend on, were formed in, relationships; 'externally', in that the system depends on, is formed in, the institutions which activate it (and which are then at once cultural and social and economic institutions); integrally, in that a 'sign-system', properly understood, is at once a specific cultural technology and a specific form of practical consciousness: those apparently diverse elements which are in fact unified in the material social process. Current work on the photograph, on the film, on the book, on painting and its reproduction, and on the 'framed flow' of television, to take only the most immediate examples, is a sociology of culture in this new dimension, from which no aspect of a process is excluded and in which the active and formative relationships of a process, right through to its still active 'products', are specifically and structurally connected: at once a 'sociology' and an 'aesthetics'.

III. Literary Theory

1. The Multiplicity of Writing

Literary theory cannot be separated from cultural theory, though it may be distinguished within it. This is the central challenge of any social theory of culture. Yet while this challenge has to be sustained at every point, in general and in detail, it is necessary to be precise about the modes of distinction which then follow. Some of these become modes of effective separation, with important theoretical and practical consequences. But there is equal danger in an opposite kind of error, in which the generalizing and connecting impulse is so strong that we lose sight of real specificities and distinctions of practice, which are then neglected or reduced to simulations of more general forms.

The theoretical problem is that two very powerful modes of distinction are deeply implanted in modern culture. These are the supposedly distinctive categories of 'literature' and of 'the aesthetic'. Each, of course, is historically specific: a formulation of bourgeois culture at a definite period of its development, from the mid-eighteenth to the mid-nineteenth century. But we cannot say this merely dismissively. In each mode of distinction, and in many of the consequent particular definitions, there are elements which cannot be surrendered, either to historical reaction or to a confused projective generalization. Rather, we have to try to analyse the very complicated pressures and limits which, in their weakest forms, these definitions falsely stabilized, yet which, in their strongest forms, they sought to emphasize as new cultural practice.

We have already examined the historical development of the concept of 'literature': from its connections with literacy to an emphasis on polite learning and on printed books, and then, in its most interesting phase, to an emphasis on 'creative' or 'imaginative' writing as a special and indispensable kind of cultural practice. It is important that elements of this new definition of literature were dragged back to older concepts, as in the attempted isolation of 'the literary tradition' as a form of the tradition of 'polite learning'. But it is more important that the most active elements of the new definition were both specialized and contained, in quite new ways.

The specialization was the interpretation of 'creative' or

'imaginative' writing through the weak and ambiguous concept of 'fiction', or through the grander but even more questionable concepts of 'imagination' and 'myth'. The containment partly followed from this specialization, but was decisively reinforced by the concept of 'criticism': in part the operative procedure of a selecting and containing 'tradition'; in part also the key shift from creativity and imagination as active productive processes to categorical abstractions demonstrated and ratified by conspicuous humanistic consumption: criticism as 'cultivation', 'discrimination', or 'taste'.

Neither the specialization nor the containment has ever been completed. Indeed, in the continuing reality of the practice of writing this is strictly impossible. But each has done significant harm, and in their domination of literary theory have become major obstacles to the understanding of both theory and practice. It is still difficult, for example, to prevent any attempt at literary theory from being turned, almost *a priori*, into critical theory, as if the only major questions about literary production were variations on the question "how do we *judge*?" At the same time, in looking at actual writing, the crippling categorizations and dichotomies of 'fact' and 'fiction', or of 'discursive' and 'imaginative' or 'referential' and 'emotive', stand regularly not only between works and readers (whence they feed back, miserably, into the complications of 'critical theory') but between writers and works, at a still active and shaping stage.

The multiplicity of writing is its second most evident characteristic, the first being its distinctive practice of the objectified material composition of language. But of course this multiplicity is a matter of interpretation as well as of fact. Indeed multiplicity can be realized in weak ways as often as strong. Where the specializing and containing categories operate at an early stage, multiplicity is little more than a recognition of varying 'forms of literature'—poetry, drama, novel—or of forms within these forms—'lyric', 'epic,' 'narrative', and so on. The point is not that these recognitions of variation are unimportant; on the contrary they are necessary, though not always in these received and often residual forms. The really severe limitation is the line drawn between all these variations and other 'non-literary' forms of writing. Pre-bourgeois categorization was normally in terms of the writing itself, as in the relatively evident distinction between verse and other forms of composition, usually drawn in characteristically feudal or aristocratic terms of 'elevation' or 'dignity'. It is significant that while that distinction held, verse normally included what would now be called 'historical' or 'philosophical' or 'descriptive' or 'didactic' or even 'instructional' writing, as well as what would now be called 'imaginative' or 'dramatic' or 'fictional' or 'personal' writing and experience.

The bourgeois drawing and redrawing of all these lines was a complex process. On the one hand it was the result, or more strictly the means, of a decisive secularization, rationalization, and eventually popularization of a wide area of experience. Different values can be attached to each of these processes at different stages, but in history, philosophy, and social and scientific description it is clear that new kinds of distinction about forms and methods of writing were radically connected with new kinds of distinction about intention. 'Elevation' and 'dignity' gave place, inevitably, in certain selected fields, to 'practicality', 'effectiveness', or 'accuracy'. Intentions other than these were either willingly conceded or contemptuously dismissed. 'Literature' as a body of 'polite learning' was still used to unite these varying intentions, but under pressure, especially in the late eighteenth and early nineteenth centuries, this broke down. 'Literature' became either the conceded or the contemptuous alternative—the sphere of imagination or fancy, or of emotional substance and effect—or, at the insistence of its practitioners, the relatively removed but again 'higher' dimension—the creative as distinguished from the rational or the practical. In this complex interaction it is of course significant that the separated literature itself changed, in many of its immediate forms. In the 'realist' novel, especially in its distinction from 'romance', in the new drama (socially extended, secular and contemporary), and in the new special forms of biography and autobiography, many of the same secular, rational, or popular impulses changed particular forms of writing from the inside, or created new literary forms.

Two major consequences followed from this. There was a falsification—false distancing—of the 'fictional' or the 'imaginary' (and connected with these the 'subjective'). And there was a related suppression of the fact of writing—active signifying composition—in what was distinguished as the 'practical', the 'factual', or the 'discursive'. These consequences are profoundly related. To move, by definition, from the 'creative' to the 'fictional', or from the 'imaginative' to the 'imaginary', is to deform the real practices of writing under the pressure of the interpretation of certain specific forms. The extreme negative definition of 'fiction' (or of 'myth')—an account of 'what did not (really) happen'—depends, evidently, on a pseudo-positive isolation of the contrasting definition, 'fact'. The real range in the major forms—epic, romance, drama, narrative—in which this question of 'fact' and 'fiction' arises is the more complex series: what really happened; what might (could) have happened; what really happens; what might happen; what essentially (typically) happened/happens. Similarly the extreme negative definition of 'imaginary persons'—'who did not/do not exist'—modulates in practice into the series: who existed in this way; who might (could) have existed; who might (could) exist; who essentially (typically) exist. The range of actual writing makes use, implicitly or explicitly, of all these propositions, but not only in the forms that are historically specialized as 'literature'. The characteristically 'difficult' forms (difficult because of the deformed definition) of history, memoir, and biography use a significant part of each series, and given the use of real characters and events in much major epic, romance, drama, and narrative, the substantial overlap—indeed in many areas the substantial community—is undeniable.

The range of actual writing similarly surpasses any reduction of 'creative imagination' to the 'subjective', with its dependent propositions: 'literature' as 'internal' or 'inner' truth; other forms of writing as 'external' truth. These depend, ultimately, on the characteristic bourgeois separation of 'individual' and 'society' and on the older idealist separation of 'mind' and 'world'. The range of writing, in most forms, crosses these artificial categories again and again, and the extremes can even be stated in an opposite way: autobiography ('what I experienced', 'what happened to me') is 'subjective' but (ideally) 'factual' writing; realist fiction or naturalist drama ('people as they are', 'the world as it is') is 'objective' (the narrator or even the fact of narrative occluded in the form) but (ideally) 'creative' writing.

The full range of writing extends even further. Argument, for example, can be distinguished from narrative or characterizing forms, but in practice certain forms of narrative (exemplary instances) or forms of characterization (this kind or person, this kind of behaviour) are radically embedded in many forms of argument. Moreover, the very fact of address—a crucial element in argument—is a *stance* (at times sustained, at times varying) strictly comparable to elements that are elsewhere isolated as narrative or dramatic. This is true even of the apparently extreme case, in which the stance is 'impersonal' (the scientific paper), where it is the practical mode of writing that establishes this (conventional) absence of personality, in the interest of the necessary creation of the 'impersonal observer'. Thus over a practical range from stance to selection, and in the employment of the vast variety of explicit or implicit propositions which define and control composition, this real multiplicity of writing is continually evident, and much of what has been known as literary theory is a way either of confusing or of diminishing it. The first task of any social theory is then to analyse the forms which have determined certain (interpreted) inclusions and certain (categorical) exclusions. Subject always to the effect of residual categorization, the development of these forms is in the end a social history. The dichotomies fact/fiction and objective/subjective are then the theoretical and historical keys to the basic bourgeois theory of literature, which has controlled and specialized the actual multiplicity of writing.

Yet there is another necessary key. The multiplicity of productive practice was in one way acknowledged, and then effectively occluded, by a transfer of interest from intention to effect. The replacement of the disciplines of grammar and rhetoric (which speak to the multiplicites of intention and performance) by the discipline of criticism (which speaks of effect, and only through effect to intention and performance) is a central intellectual movement of the bourgeois period. Each kind of discipline moved, in the period of change, to a particular pole: grammar and rhetoric to writing; criticism to reading. Any social theory, by contrast, requires the activation of both poles: not merely their interaction—movement from one fixed point, stance, or intention to and from another; but their profound interlocking in actual composition. Something of this kind is now being attempted in what is known (but residually) as communication theory and aesthetics.

And it is on the delineation of 'aesthetics' that we have first to fix our attention. From the description of a theory of perception aesthetics became, in the eighteenth and especially the nineteenth century, a new specializing form of description of the response to 'art' (itself newly generalized from skill to 'imaginative' skill). What emerged in bourgeois economics as the 'consumer'—the abstract figure corresponding to the abstraction of (market and commodity) 'production'—emerged in cultural theory as 'aesthetics' and 'the aesthetic response'. All problems of the multiplicities of intention and performance could then be undercut, or bypassed, by the transfer of energy to this other pole. Art, including literature, was to be defined by its capacity to evoke this special response: initially the perception of beauty; then the pure contemplation of an object, for its own sake and without other ('external') considerations; then also the perception and contemplation of the 'making' of an object: its language, its skill of construction, its 'aesthetic properties'. Such response (power to evoke response) could be as present in a work of history or philosophy as in a play or poem or novel (and all were then 'literature'). Equally, it could be absent in this play or this poem or this novel (and these were then 'not literature' or 'not really literature' or 'bad literature'). The specializing concept of 'literature', in its modern forms, is thus a central example of the controlling and categorizing specialization of 'the aesthetic'.

2. Aesthetic and other Situations

Yet it is clear, historically, that the definition of 'aesthetic' response is an affirmation, directly comparable with the definition and affirmation of 'creative imagination', of certain human meanings and values which a dominant social system reduced and even tried to exclude. Its history is in large part a protest against the forcing of all experience into instrumentality ('utility'), and of all things into commodities. This must be remembered even as we add, necessarily, that the form of this protest, within definite social and historical conditions, led almost inevitably to new kinds of privileged instrumentality and specialized commodity. The humane response was nevertheless there. It has remained important, and still necessary, in controversies within twentieth-century Marxism, where, for example, the (residual bourgeois) reduction of art to social engineering ('ideology') or superstructural reflection (simple 'realism') has been opposed by a tendency, centred on Lukács, to distinguish and defend 'the specificity of the aesthetic'. ('Specificity' is used to translate Lukács's key term *kulonosség*—Hungarian— or *besonderheit*— German; the translation, as Fekete (1972) has shown, is difficult, and 'speciality' and 'particularity', which have both been used, are misleading; Fekete's own translation is 'peculiarity'.)

Lukács sought to define art in ways which would distinguish it, categorically, from both the 'practical' and the 'magical'. 'Practical', here, is seen as limited by its containment within specific historical forms: for example, the reduced practice of capitalist society, which is ordinarily reified as 'reality' and to which art is then a necessary alternative. (This repeats, as often in Lukács, the radical idealism of the beginnings of this movement). But, equally, the aesthetic must be distinguished from the 'magical' or 'religious'. These offer their images as objectively real, transcendent, and demanding belief. Art offers its images as images, closed and real in themselves (following a familiar isolation of the 'aesthetic'), but at the same time represents a *human* generality: a real mediation between (isolated) subjectivity and (abstract) universality; a specific process of the 'identical subject/object'.

152   **Marxism and Literature**

This definition is the strongest contemporary form of the affirmation of genuine 'aesthetic' practice as against a reduced 'practicality' or a displaced 'myth-making'. But it raises fundamental problems. It is, intrinsically, a categorical proposition, defensible at that level but immediately subject to major difficulties when it is taken into the multiple world of social and cultural process. Indeed its difficulties are similar to those which confronted formalism after its critical attempt to isolate the art-object as a thing in itself, to be examined only in its own terms and through its own 'means' or 'devices': an attempt founded on the hypothesis of a specifically distinguishable 'poetic language'. It is never the categorical distinction between aesthetic intentions, means, and effects and other intentions, means, and effects which presents difficulties. The problem is to sustain such a distinction through the inevitable extension to an indissoluble social material process: not only indissoluble in the social conditions of the making and reception of art, within a general social process from which these can not be excised; but also indissoluble in the actual making and reception, which are connecting material processes within a social system of the use and transformation of material (including language) by material means. The formalists, seeking 'specificity', in their detailed studies, not in a category but in what they claimed to show as a specific 'poetic language', reached this crucial impasse earlier and more openly. One way out (or back) was the conversion of all social and cultural practice to 'aesthetic' forms in this sense: a solution, or displacement, since widely evident in the 'closed forms' of structuralist linguistics and in structuralist-semiotic literary and cultural studies. Another and more interesting way out was to move definition of the aesthetic to a 'function', and therefore a 'practice', as distinct from its location in special objects or special means.

The best repesentative of this more interesting apparent solution is Mukarovsky; for example in his *Aesthetic Function, Norm and Value as Social Facts*. Mukarovsky, facing the multiplicity of practice, had little difficulty in showing that

there are no objects or actions which, by virtue of their essence or organization would, regardless of time, place or the person evaluating them, possess an aesthetic function, and others which, again by their very nature, would be necessarily immune to the aesthetic function. (p. 1)

He took examples not only from the recognized arts, in which the aesthetic function which appears to be their primary definition may be displaced and overridden, or destroyed and lost, but also from the 'borderline' cases of the decorative arts, craft production, the continuum of processes in building and architecture, landscape, social manners, the preparation and presentation of food and drink, and the varied functions of dress. He conceded that there are

— within art and outside of it—objects which, by virtue of their organization are meant to have an aesthetic effect. This is actually the essential property of art. But an active capacity for the aesthetic function is not a real property of an object, even if the object has been deliberately composed with the aesthetic function in mind. Rather, the aesthetic function manifests itself only under certain conditions, i.e. in a certain social context. (p. 3)

What then is the aesthetic function? Mukarovsky's elaborately differentiated argument ends in the radical diversification of what had been singular terms, which yet he retains. Art is not a special kind of object but one in which the aesthetic function, usually mixed with other functions, is *dominant*. Art, with other things (landscape and dress, most evidently), gives aesthetic pleasure, but this cannot be transliterated as a sense of beauty or a sense of perceived form, since while these are central in the aesthetic function they are historically and socially variable, and in all real instances concrete. At the same time the aesthetic function is "not an epiphenomenon of other functions" but a "codeterminant of human reaction to reality".

Mukarovsky's important work is best seen as the penultimate stage of the critical dissolution of the specializing and controlling categories of bourgeois aesthetic theory. Almost all the original advantages of this theory have been quite properly, indeed necessarily, abandoned. 'Art' as a categorically separate dimension, or body of objects; 'the aesthetic' as an isolable extra-social phenomenon: each has been broken up by a return to the variability, the relativity, and the multiplicity of actual cultural practice. We can then see more clearly the ideological function of the specializing abstractions of 'art' and 'the aesthetic'. What they represent, in an abstract way, is a particular stage of the division of labour. 'Art' is a kind of production which has to be seen as separate from the dominant bourgeois productive norm: the making of commodities. It has then, in fantasy, to be separated from 'production' altogether; described by the new term 'creation'; distinguished from its own material processes; distinguished, finally, from other products of its own kind or closely related kinds—'art' from 'non-art'; 'literature' from 'para-literature' or 'popular literature'; 'culture' from 'mass culture'. The narrowing abstraction is then so powerful that, in its name, we find ways of neglecting (or of dismissing as peripheral) that relentless transformation of art works into commodities, within the dominant forms of capitalist society. Art and thinking about art have to separate themselves, by ever more absolute abstraction, from the social processes within which they are still contained. Aesthetic theory is the main instrument of this evasion. In its concentration on receptive states, on psychological responses of an abstractly differentiated kind, it represents the division of labour in consumption corresponding to the abstraction of art as the division of labour in production.

Mukarovsky, from within this tradition, in effect destroyed it. He restored real connections even while retaining the terms of the deliberate disconnection. Aesthetic function, aesthetic norms, aesthetic values: each in turn was scrupulously followed through to historical social practice, yet each, as a category, was almost desperately retained. The reason is evident. While the dominant elements of human practice, within a specific and dominant form of society, exclude or undervalue known and pressing elements of human intention and response, a specialized and privileged area—'art' and 'the aesthetic'—has, it can seem, to be defined and defended, even after the point at which it is realized that interrelationship and interpenetration are radically inevitable: the point at which the 'area' is redefined as a 'function'.

The next step in the argument has now to be taken. What Mukarovsky abstracted as a function has to be seen, rather, as a series of situations, in which specific intentions and responses combine, within discoverable formations, to produce a true range of specific facts and effects. It is obvious that one primary feature of such situations is the availability of works which are specifically designed to occasion them, and of specific institutions which are intended to be such actual occasions; (an *occasion*, however, is only potentially a *function*). Yet such situations are still, as history shows us, highly variable and commonly mixed, and the works and institutions vary accordingly. It is in this sense that we have to replace the specializing category of 'the aesthetic', and its dependent and circulating categories of 'the arts', by the radically different vocabulary of 'the dominant', the 'associated', and the 'subordinate' which, in the last phase of rigorous specialization, the formalists and the social formalists necessarily developed. What the formalists saw as a hierarchy within specific forms, and the social formalists as a hierarchy of specific practices, has to be extended to the area in which these hierarchies are both determined and contested: the full social material process itself.

Apart from the complications of received theory, this is not really difficult. Anyone who is in contact with the real multiplicity of writing, and with the no less real multiplicity of those forms of writing that have been specialized as literature, is already aware of the range of intentions and responses which are continually and variably manifest and latent. The honest muddle that so often arises is a consequence of pressure from both ends of a range of received and incompatible theories. If we are asked to believe that all literature is 'ideology', in the crude sense that its dominant intention (and then our only response) is the communication or imposition of 'social' or 'political' meanings and values, we can only, in the end, turn away. If we are asked to believe that all literature is 'aesthetic', in the crude sense that its dominant intention (and then our only response) is the beauty of language or form, we may stay a little longer but will still in the end turn away. Some people will lurch from one position to the other. More, in practice, will retreat to an indifferent acknowledgement of complexity, or assert the autonomy of their own (usually consensual) response.

But it is really much simpler to face the facts of the range of intentions and effects, and to face it *as a range*. All writing carries references, meanings, and values. To suppress or displace them is in the end impossible. But to say 'all writing carries' is only a way of saying that language and form are constitutive processes of reference, meaning, and value, and that these are not necessarily identical with, or exhausted by, the kinds of reference, meaning, and value that correspond or can be grouped with generalized references, meanings and values that are also evident, in other senses and in summary, elsewhere.

This recognition is lost if it is specialized to 'beauty', though to suppress or displace the real experience to which that abstraction points is also in the end impossible. The true effects of many kinds of writing are indeed quite physical: specific alterations of physical rhythms, physical organization: experiences of quickening and slowing, of expansion and of intensification. It was to these experiences, more varied and more intricate than any general naming can indicate, that the categorization of 'the aesthetic' appeared to speak, and that the reduction to 'ideology' tried and failed to deny or make incidental. Yet the categorization was complicit with a deliberately dividing society, and could then not admit what is also evident: the dulling, the lulling, the chiming, the overbearing, which are also, in real terms, 'aesthetic' experiences: aesthetic effects but also aesthetic intentions. What we can practically though variably recognize in specific works has to be linked with the complex formations, situations, and occasions in which such intentions and such responses are made possible, are modified, and are encouraged or deflected.

Thus we have to reject 'the aesthetic' both as a separate abstract dimension and as a separate abstract function. We have to reject 'Aesthetics' to the large extent that it is posited on these abstractions. At the same time we have to recognize and indeed emphasize the specific variable intentions and the specific variable responses that have been grouped as aesthetic in distinction from other isolated intentions and responses, and in particular from information and suasion, in their simplest senses. Indeed, we cannot rule out, theoretically, the possibility of discovering certain invariant combinations of elements within this grouping, even while we recognize that such invariant combinations as have hitherto been described depend on evident processes of supra-historical appropriation and selection. Moreover, the grouping is not a way of assigning value, even relative value. Any concentration on language or form, in sustained or temporary priority over other elements and other ways of realizing meaning and value, is specific: at times an intense and irreplaceable experience in which these fundamental elements of human process are directly stimulated, reinforced, or extended; at times, at a different extreme, an evasion of other immediate connections, an evacuation of immediate situation, or a privileged indifference to the human process as a whole. ("Does a man die at your feet, your business is not to help him, but to note the colour of his lips.")*

Value cannot reside in the concentration or in the priority or in the elements which provoke these. The argument of values is in the *variable* encounters of intention and response in *specific situations*. The key to any analysis, and from analysis back to theory, is then the recognition of precise situations in which what have been isolated, and displaced, as 'the aesthetic intention' and 'the aesthetic response' have occurred. Such 'situations' are not only 'moments.' In the varied historical development of human culture they are almost continuously both organized and disorganized, with precise but highly variable formations initiating, sustaining, enclosing, or destroying them. The history of such formations is the specific and highly varied history of art. Yet to enter any part of this history, in an active way, we have to learn to understand the specific elements—conventions and notations—which are the material keys to intention and response, and, more generally, the specific elements which socially and historically determine and signify aesthetic and other situations.

* John Ruskin in the manuscript printed as an Appendix to *Modern Painters* (Library Edition, London, 1903–12), ii. 388–9.

3. From Medium to Social Practice

Any description of 'situations' is manifestly social, but as a description of cultural practice it is still evidently incomplete. What is ordinarily added (or what in an earlier and persistent kind of theory was taken as definitive) is a specification of cultural practice in terms of its 'medium'. Literature, it is said, is a particular kind of work in the medium of language. Anything else, though important, is peripheral to this: a situation in which the real work is begun, or in which it is received. The work itself is in 'the medium'.

Some emphasis of this kind is indeed necessary, but we have to look very carefully at its definition as work in a 'medium'. We saw earlier the inherent dualism in the idea of 'mediation', but in most of its uses it continues to denote an activity: an active relationship or, more interestingly, a specific transformation of material. What is interesting about 'medium' is that it began as a definition of an activity by an apparently autonomous object or force. This was particularly clear when the word acquired the first element of its modern sense in the early seventeenth century. Thus 'to the Sight three things are required, the Object, the Organ and the Medium'. Here a description of the practical activity of seeing, which is a whole and complex process of relationship between the developed organs of sight and the accessible properties of things seen, is characteristically interrupted by the invention of a third term which is given its own properties, in abstraction from the practical relationship. This general notion of intervening and in effect causal substances, on which various practical operations were believed to depend, had a long course in scientific thought, down to 'phlogiston' and 'caloric'. But in the case of a hypothetical substance, in some natural operation, it was accessible to and could be corrected by continued observation.

It was a different matter when the same hypothesis was applied to human activities, and especially to language. Bacon wrote of thoughts 'expressed by the Medium of Wordes', and this is an example of the familiar position, already examined, in which thoughts exist before language and are then expressed through its 'medium'. A constitutive human activity is thus abstracted and objectified. Words are seen as objects, things, which men take up and arrange into particular forms to express or communicate information which, before this work in the 'medium', they already possess. This notion, in many different forms, has persisted even into some modern communications theory. It reaches its extreme in the assumption of the independent properties of the 'medium', which, in one kind of theory, is seen as determining not only the 'content' of what is communicated but also the social relationships within which the communication takes place. In this influential kind of technological determinism (for example, in McLuhan) the 'medium' is (metaphysically) the master.

Two other developments in the idea of a 'medium' must also be noted. From the eighteenth century it was often used to describe what we would now ordinarily call a means of communication. It was particularly used of newspapers: "through the medium . . . of your publication"; "your Journal one of the best possible mediums". In the twentieth century, the description of a newspaper as a 'medium' for advertising became common, and the extended description of the press and broadcasting as 'the media' was affected by this. 'A medium' or 'the media' is then, on the one hand, a term for a social organ or institution of general communication—a relatively neutral use—and, on the other hand, a term for a secondary or derived use (as in advertising) of an organ or institution with another apparently primary purpose. Yet in either case the 'medium' is a form of social organization, something essentially different from the idea of an intermediate communicative substance.

However, the notion of an intermediate substance was also extensively and simultaneously developed, especially in the visual arts: 'the medium of oils' or 'the medium of water-colour': in fact as a development from a relatively neutral scientific sense of the carrier of some active substance. The 'medium' in painting had been any liquid with which pigments could be mixed; it was then extended to the active mixture and so to the specific practice. There was then an important extended use in all the arts. 'Medium' became the specific material with which a particular kind of artist worked. To understand this 'medium' was obviously a condition of professional skill and practice. Thus far there was not, and is not, any real difficulty. But a familiar process of reification occurred, reinforced by the influence of formalism. The properties of 'the medium' were abstracted as if they defined the practice, rather than being its means. This interpretation then suppressed the full sense of practice, which has always to be defined as work on a material for a specific purpose within certain necessary social conditions. Yet this real practice is easily displaced (often by only a small extension from the necessary emphasis on knowing how to handle the material) to an activity defined, not by the material, which would be altogether too crude, but by that particular projection and reification of work on the material which is called 'the medium'.

Yet this is still a projection and reification of a practical operation. Even in this diminished form, concentration on 'the medium', as at least the location of a process of work, is very much preferable to those conceptions of 'art' which had become almost wholly divorced from its original general sense of skilled work (as 'poetry' had also been moved from a sense which contained a central emphasis on 'making' and 'the maker'). In fact the two processes— the idealization of art and the reification of the medium— were connected, through a specific and strange historical development. Art was idealized to distinguish it from 'mechanical' work. One motive, undoubtedly, was a simple class emphasis, to separate 'higher' things—the objects of interest to free men, the 'liberal arts'—from the 'ordinary' business ('mechanical' as manual work, and then as work with machines) of the 'everyday world'. A later phase of the idealization, however, was a form of oblique (and sometimes direct) protest against what work had become, within capitalist production. An early manifesto of English Romanticism, Young's *Conjectures on Original Composition* (1759), defined original art as rising

spontaneously from the vital root of genius; it *grows*, it is not made. Imitations are often a sort of *manufacture*, wrought up by those *mechanics*, *art* and *labour*, out of pre-existent materials not their own.

From a similar position Blake attacked

the Monopolizing Trader who Manufactures Art by the Hands of Ignorant Journeymen till . . . he is Counted the Greatest Genius who can sell a Good-for-Nothing Commodity for a Great Price.

All the traditional terms were now in fact confused, under the pressure of changes in the general mode of production, and the steady extension of these changes to the production of 'art', when both art and knowledge, as Adam Smith realistically observed, were

purchased, in the same manner as shoes or stockings, from those whose business it is to make up and prepare for the market that particular species of goods.

Both the dominant bourgeois definition of work as the production of commodities, and the steady practical inclusion of works of art as commodities among others, led to this special form of a general protest.

A practical alienation was being radically experienced, at two interconnecting levels. There was the loss of connection between a worker's own purposes, and thus his 'original' identity, and the actual work he was hired to perform. There was also the loss of the 'work' itself, which when it was made, within this mode of production, necessarily became a commodity. The protest in the name of 'art' was then at one level the protest of craftsmen—most of them literally hand-craftsmen—against a mode of production which steadily excluded them or profoundly altered their status. But at another level it was a claim for a significant meaning of work—that of using human energy on material for an autonomous purpose—which was being radically displaced and denied, in most kinds of production, but which could be more readily and more confidently asserted, in the case of art, by association with the 'life of the spirit' or 'our general humanity'.

The argument was eventually consciously articulated and generally applied by William Morris. But the orthodox development of the original perception was an idealization, in which 'art' was exempted from, made exceptional to, what 'work' had been made to mean. At the same time, however, no artist could dispense with his working skills. Still, as before, the making of art was experienced, tangibly, as a craft, a skill, a long working process. The special senses of 'medium' were then exceptionally reinforced: medium as intermediate agency, between an 'artistic impulse' and a complete 'work'; or medium as the objectified properties of the working process itself. To have seen the working process differently, not with the specializing senses of 'medium', but as a particular case of conscious practice, and thus 'practical consciousness', would have endangered the precious reservation of art from the conditions, not only of practical everyday work—that relation which had once, in a different social order, been accepted—but of the capitalist system of material production for a market.

Yet painters and sculptors remained manual workers. Musicians remained involved with the material performance and material notation of instruments which were the products of conscious and prolonged manual skills. Dramatists remained involved with the material properties of stages and the physical properties of actors and voices. Writers, in ways which we must examine and distinguish, handled material notations on paper. Necessarily, inside any art, there is this physical and material consciousness. It is only when the working process and its results are seen or interpreted in the degraded forms of material commodity production that the significant protest—the denial of materiality by these necessary workers with material—is made and projected into abstracted 'higher' or 'spiritual' forms. The protest is understandable, but these 'higher' forms of production, embodying many of the most intense and most significant forms of human experience, are more clearly understood when they are recognized as specific objectifications, in relatively durable material organizations, of what are otherwise the least durable though often the most powerful and affective human moments. The inescapable materiality of works of art is then the irreplaceable materialization of kinds of experience, including experience of the production of objects, which, from our deepest sociality, go beyond not only the production of commodities but also our ordinary experience of objects.

At the same time, beyond this, material cultural production has a specific social history. Much of the evident crisis of 'literature', in the second half of the twentieth century, is the result of altered processes and relationships in basic material produc-'ion. I do not mean only the radical material changes in printing ـnd publishing, though these have had direct effects. I mean also the development of new material forms of dramatization and narrative in the specific technologies of motion pictures, sound broadcasting, and television, involving not only new intrinsic material processes, which in the more complex technologies bring with them quite new problems of material notation and realization, but also new working relationships on which the complex technologies depend. In one phase of material literary production, most typically from the seventeenth to the mid-twentieth century, the author was a solitary handworker, alone with his 'medium'. Subsequent material processes—printing and distribution—could then be seen as simple accessories. But in other phases, earlier and later, the work was from the beginning undertaken in relation with others (for example in the Elizabethan theatre or in a motion-picture or broadcasting unit) and the immediate material process was more than notation as a stage of transcription or publication. It was, and is, co-operative material production involving many processes of a material and physical kind. The reservation of 'literature' to the specific technology of pen and paper, linked to the printed book, is then an important historical phase, but not, in relation to the many practices which it offers to represent, any kind of absolute definition.

Yet these are not, except in a kind of shorthand, problems of 'the medium' or of 'new media'. Every specific art has dissolved into it, at every level of its operations, not only specific social relationships, which in a given phase define it (even at its most apparently solitary), but also specific material means of production, on the mastery of which its production depends. It is because they are dissolved that they are not 'media'. The form of social relationship and the form of material production are specifically linked. Not always, however, in some simple identity. The contradiction between an increasingly collaborative production and the learned skills and values of individual production is now especially acute in several kinds of writing (the dramatic most evidently, but also much narrative and argument), and not only as a publishing or distributing problem, as which it is often most identifiable, but right back in the processes of writing itself.

Significantly, since the late nineteenth century, crises of technique—which can be isolated as problems of the 'medium' or of the 'form'—have been directly linked with a sense of crisis in the relationship of art to society, or in the very purposes of art which had previously been agreed or even taken for granted. A new technique has often been seen, realistically, as a new relationship, or as depending on a new relationship. Thus what had been isolated as a medium, in many ways rightly as a way of emphasizing the material production which any art must be, came to be seen, inevitably, as social practice; or, in the crisis of modern cultural production, as a crisis of social practice. This is the crucial common factor, in otherwise diverse tendencies, which links the radical aesthetics of modernism and the revolutionary theory and practice of Marxism.

4. Signs and Notations

Language, then, is not a medium; it is a constitutive element of material social practice. But if this is so, it is clearly also a special case. For it is at once a material practice and a process in which many complex activities, of a less manifestly material kind—from information to interaction, from representation to imagination, and from abstract thought to immediate emotion—are specifically realized. Language is in fact a special kind of material practice: that of human sociality. And then, to the extent that material practice is limited to the production of objects, or that social practice is taken to exclude or to contrast with individual practice, language can become unrecognizable in its real forms. Within this failure of recognition, alternative partial accounts of language are made the basis of, among other matters, alternative kinds of literary theory. The two major alternative kinds, in our own culture, are on the one hand 'expressivism', in its simple forms of 'psychological realism' or the writing of 'personal experience', or its disguised forms of naturalism and simple realism—expressing the truth of an observed situation or fact—and on the other hand, 'formalism', in its variants of instances of a form, assemblies of literary devices, or 'texts' of a 'system of signs'. Each of these general theories grasps real elements of the practice of writing, but commonly in ways which deny other real elements and even make them inconceivable.

Thus formalism focuses our attention on what is evidently present and might well be overlooked in writing: the specific and definitive uses of literary forms of many kinds, from the most general to the most local, which have always to be seen as more than simple 'vehicles' or 'scaffolding' for the expression of an independent experience. At the same time it deflects our attention, and in doing so becomes incredible beyond certain limited circles, from the more than formal meanings and values, and in this sense the defining experiences, of almost all actual works. The impatient 'commonsense' reaction, that literature does, quite evidently, describe events, depict situations, express the experiences of real men and women, is in this context understandable and persuasive. Yet the reaction is still not a possible literary theory, that is to say, a consciousness of real literary practice. We have to learn to look in the space between the deflection and the reaction if we are to grasp the significance of the practice as a whole. What we then find is that we have been dealing with complementary errors.

The central error of expressivist theory—an error common to descriptions of naturalism or simple realism and to descriptions of psychological realism or literature as personal experience (descriptions which are in fact often opposed to each other and which contend for significance and priority)—is the failure to acknowledge the fact that meaning is always *produced*; it is never simply expressed.

There are indeed crucial variations in the methods of its production, from a relatively complete reliance on already established meanings and interrelations of meanings to a relatively complete reworking of available meanings and the discovery of new combinations of meanings. In fact neither of these methods is as complete, as self-contained, as it may at first sight appear. The 'orthodox' work is still always a specific production. 'Experimental' work depends, even predominantly, on a shared consciousness of already available meanings. For these are the defining characteristics and then the real determinations of the process of language as such. No expression, that is to say—no account, description, depiction, portrait—is 'natural' or 'straightforward'. These are at most socially relative terms. Language is not a pure medium through which the reality of a life or the reality of an event or an experience or the reality of a society can 'flow'. It is a socially shared and reciprocal activity, already embedded in active relationships, within which every move is an activation of what is already shared and reciprocal or may become so.

Thus to address an account to another is, explicitly or potentially, as in any act of expression, to evoke or propose a relationship. It is also, through this, to evoke or propose an active relationship to the experience being expressed, whether this condition of relationship is seen as the truth of a real event or the significance of an imagined event, the reality of a social situation or the significance of a response to it, the reality of a private experience or the significance of its imaginative projection, or the reality of some part of the physical world or the significance of some element of perception or response to it.

Every expression proposes this complex relationship, on which, but to variable degrees of consciousness and conscious attention, it depends. It is then important that the complex relationship implicit in any expression should not be reduced to categorical or general (for example, abstracted political and economic) factors, as some of the simpler Marxist theories propose. But it remains essential to grasp the full social significance that is always *active and inherent* in any apparently 'natural' or 'straightforward' account. Crucial assumptions and propositions, not simply in ideology or in conscious stance, but in the ebb and flow of feeling from and to others, in assumed situations and relationships, and in the relationships implied or proposed within the immediate uses of language, are always present and are always directly significant. In many instances, and especially in class-divided societies, it is necessary to make them explicit, by analysis, and to show, in detail, that this is not a case of going 'beyond' the literary work, but of going more thoroughly into its full (and not arbitrarily protected) expressive significance.

It was a version of this procedure which one tendency in formalism proposed. Other variants of formalism underlined the general forms within which particular expressions occurred, or drew attention to the devices, seen as active elements of form or formation, through which presentation of the expression was effected. A more radical formalism, reacting against notions of language and expression as 'natural', reduced the whole process to what it saw as its basic constituents; to 'signs', and then to a 'system of signs', concepts which it had borrowed from one kind of linguistics (see I, 2 above).

The sense of a *production* of meanings was then notably strengthened. Any unit of expression can be shown, by analysis, to depend on the formal signs which are words and not persons or things, and on their formal arrangement. 'Natural' expression of 'reality' or 'experience' can be convincingly shown to be a myth, occluding this real and demonstrable activity. Yet what then usually happened was the production (itself not scrutinized) of a new myth, based on the following assumptions: that all 'signs' are arbitrary; that the 'system of signs' is determined by its formal internal relations; that 'expression' is not only not 'natural' but is a form of 'codification'; and that the appropriate response to 'codification' is 'decipherment', 'deconstruction'. Each of these assumptions is in fact ideological, to be sure in response to another and more pervasive ideology.

For the 'sign' is 'arbitrary' only from a position of conscious or unconscious alienation. Its apparent arbitrariness is a form of social distance, itself a form of relationship. The social history of philology and of comparative linguistics, based so largely in residual or in colonizing formations, prepared the way for this alienation, and, ironically, naturalized it. Every expression, every utterance, is within its procedures an 'alien' fact. The formal quality of words as 'signs', which was correctly perceived, was rendered as 'arbitrary' by a privileged withdrawal from the lived and living relationships which, within any native language (the languages of real societies, to which all men belong), *make all formal meanings significant and substantial*, in a world of reciprocal reference which moves, as it must, beyond the signs. To reduce words to 'arbitrary' signs, and to reduce language to a 'system' of signs, is then either a realized alienation (the position of the alien observer of another people's language or of the conscious linguist deliberately abstracting lived and living forms for scientific analysis) or an unrealized alienation, in which a specific group, for understandable reasons, overlooks its privileged relationship to the real and active language and society all around it and in fact within it, and projects onto the activities of others its own forms of alienation. There is a respectable variant of this latter position, in which the society or form of society within which the privileged group operates is seen as 'alienated', in Marxist or post-Marxist terms, and the 'arbitrary' signs and the 'codes' they compose are seen as forms of bourgeois society. But even this is unacceptable because the theoretical assumptions within which the diagnosis is made—the arbitrariness of all 'signs', for example—are fundamentally incompatible with recognition of any *specific* kinds of alienation. Indeed, what really follows is the universality of alienation, the position of a closely associated bourgeois idealist formation, drawing its assumptions from a universalist (mainly Freudian) psychology.

Again, if a 'system of signs' has only internal formal rules, there can be no specific social formations, in historical or sociological terms, to institute, vary, or alter this kind of (social) practice. Nor, finally, can there be full social practice of any kind. The description of active practice in language as 'codification', while appearing to point to the relationships and references which the description of 'natural' expression occludes, then in its own way occludes them, by withdrawing attention from a continuous and varied material social practice, and rendering all this practice into formal terms. 'Code' has a further irony, in that it implies, somewhere, the existence of the same message 'in clear'. But this, even as a formal account of language, is radically wrong, and the simple notion of 'decoding' the messages of others is then a privileged fantasy. The (alienated) reference to the 'science' of such deconstruction is a displacement from the social situation, in which specific formations, and specific individuals, in highly differential but discoverable ways, are all (including the decoders) using, offering, testing, amending, and altering this central and substantial element of *their own* material and social relationships. To occlude these relationships, by reducing their expressed forms to a linguistic system, is a kind of error closely related, in effect, to that made by the theorist of 'pure' expression, for whom, also, there was no materially and socially differential world of lived and living practice; a human world of which language, in and through its own forms, is itself always a form.

To understand the materiality of language we have of course to distinguish between spoken words and written notations. This distinction, which the concept of 'sign' fundamentally obscures, has to be related to a development in means of production. Spoken words are a process of human activity using only immediate, constitutive, physical resources. Written words, with their continuing but not necessarily direct relation to speech, are a form of material production, adapting non-human resources to a human end.

There are now intermediate cases, in the mechanical and electronic recording, reproduction, and composition of speech, yet these are not, of course, notations, though difficult problems of notation are at times involved in their preparation. But the central characteristic of writing is the production of material notations, though the purposes and therefore the means of production are variable. Thus the written play is a notation of intended speech, and sometimes also of intended movement and scene (I have analysed these variations in *Drama in Performance*). Some written forms are a record of speech, or a text for speech, (speeches, lectures, sermons). But the characteristic 'literary' form is written notation for reading. It is characteristic of such notations, in printing obviously but also in copying, that they are reproducible. They are unlike normal forms of produced material objects, even such related forms as paintings. For their essential material existence is in the reproducible notations, which are then radically dependent on the cultural system within which the notations are current, as well as, in a secondary way, on the social and economic system within which they are distributed. It is thus in the whole and complex process of notation that we find the reality of this specific material and social process. Once again the linguistic elements are not signs; they are the notations of actual productive relationships.

The most basic kind of notation is of course the alphabetic. In highly literate cultures this means of production is in effect almost naturalized, but the more we learn about the processes of reading the more we realize the active and interactive relationship which this apparently settled kind of notation involves. Thus the notation is not, even at this level, simple transfer; it depends upon the active grasping, often by repeated trial and error, of shapes and relationships which the notation promotes but does not guarantee. Reading, then, is as active as writing, and the notation, as means of production, depends on both these activities and upon their effective relationship. What is true but general at this basic level remains true but highly specific in more specifying forms of notation within this general process.

Consider, for example, the complex notations of *source*: the indications, at times quite direct, at times highly indirect, of the *identity* of the writer, in all its possible senses. Such notations are often closely involved with indications of situation, the combinations of situation and identity often constituting crucial notations of part of the relationship into which the writing is intended to enter. The process of reading, in anything more than its most literal sense, is radically dependent on these indications: not only as an answer to the necessary question, 'who "speaks"?', but as answers to the necessary range of related questions: 'from what situation?'; 'with what authority?'; 'with what intention?'.

Such questions are often answered by technical analysis: the identification of 'devices'. But the technical observations—

whether arrived at analytically or, as much more commonly, through the understanding of conventional indications within a shared culture—are always methods of establishing, in what is really a simultaneous movement, the nature of the specific productive process and of the inherent relationship which it proposes. The indications may be very general; to show whether we are reading novel, biography, autobiography, memoir, or historical account. But many of the most significant notations are particular: indications of speech, reported speech and dialogue; indications of explicit and implicit thought processes; indications of displaced or suspended monologue, dialogue, or thought; indications of direct or of 'characterized' observation. All extended reading and all developed writing depend on an understanding of the range of these indications, and the indications depend on both received and possible relationships, locally materialized by processes of complex notation. And this is to see the matter only at the level of the specification of persons, events, and experiences. Some of the most important notations are indications of writing for reading in more immediate ways, within the productive process itself. Notations of order, arrangement, and the mutual relationship of parts; notations of pause, of break, of transition; notations of emphasis: all these can be said to control, but are better described as ways of realizing, the process of the specific productive relationship that is at once, in its character as notation, a way of writing and a way of reading.

It was the specific contribution of formalist studies, as of a much older tradition of rhetoric, to identify and to demonstrate the operation of such notations. At the same time, by reducing them to elements of a formal system, they occluded the extending relationships of which these elements are always and inevitably the productive means. Expressivist studies, on the other hand, reduced notations, where they noticed them at all, to mechanical elements—means to other ends—or to elements of decoration or the simple formalities of address. To the extent that this can sustain attention to the full human experiences and relationships which are in fact always in process in and through the notations, it can seem the lesser error. But the errors of each tendency are complementary, and can be corrected only by a fully social theory of literature. For the notations are relationships, expressed, offered, tested, and amended in a whole social process, in which device, expression, and the substance of expression are in the end inseparable. To look at this conclusion in another way, we must look at the nature of literary conventions.

5. Conventions

The meaning of convention was originally an assembly and then, by derivation, an agreement. Later the sense of agreement was extended to tacit agreement and thence to custom. An adverse sense developed, in which a convention was seen as no more than an old rule, or somebody else's rule, which it was proper and often necessary to disregard. The meaning of 'convention' in art and literature is still radically affected by this varying history of the word.

Yet the point is not to choose between the relatively favourable and unfavourable senses. Within any social theory of art and literature, a convention is an established relationship, or ground of a relationship, through which a specific shared practice—the making of actual works—can be realized. It is the local or general indicator, both of the situations and occasions of art, and of the means of an art. A social theory, with its emphasis on distinct and contrasting traditions, institutions, and formations, related to but not identical with distinct and opposing social classes, is thus well placed to understand the shifting evaluations of conventions and of the reality of conventions. Negatively it can uncover the characteristic belief of certain classes, institutions, and formations that their interests and procedures are not artificial and limited but universally valid and applicable, their methods then being 'true', 'real', or 'natural' as distinct from the limited and limiting 'conventions' of others. Positively it can show the real grounds of the inclusions and exclusions, the styles and the ways of seeing, that specific conventions embody and ratify. For a social theory insists on seeing, within all established relationships and procedures, the specific substance and its methods, rather than an assumed or claimed 'self-evidence' or universality.

Conventions are in this sense inherent, and by definition are historically variable. This does not mean, however, that certain kinds of convention do not extend beyond their period, class, or formation. Some fundamental literary conventions do so extend, and are crucial to problems of genre and form. Moreover, we need to define the complex relation between conventions and notations. For while all notations are conventional, not all conventions are specific notations. Notations, while obviously more specific, are also more limited than conventions, which can include, for example, conventions of the absence or the setting aside of certain procedures and substance which other conventions include. Indeed, without such conventions, many notations would be incomplete or even incomprehensible.

Certain basic conventions become in effect naturalized within a particular cultural tradition. This is true, for example, of the basic convention of dramatic performance, with its assigned distribution of actors and spectators. Within a culture in which drama is now conventional, the distribution seems self-evident and the restraints are normally respected. Outside such a culture, or at its edges, the represented dramatic action may be taken as a 'real' act, or spectators may try to intervene, beyond the conventional restraints. Even within a culture with a long tradition of drama, comparable responses, putting the conventions under pressure, are common. For dramatic performance is a convention instituted in specific periods within specific cultures, rather than any kind of 'natural' behaviour. Similar deep conventions, involving agreed relationships, apply to most kinds of oral narrative and address. Authorial identification, in drama and in printed books, is similarly subject to historically variable conventions which determine the whole concept of composition.

Moreover, within these fundamental conventions, every element of composition is also conventional, with significant historical variations in different periods and cultures, both between conventions and between their relative unity and relative diversity. Thus *basic modes of 'speech'*—from choral to individual singing to recitative to declamation to rehearsed conversation—or *of writing*—from the range of verse forms to the forms of prose, and from the 'monologic' to the 'collective'—and then the diversity of each in relation to contemporary 'everyday' spoken forms, are radically conventional. They are in many cases but not all indicated by specific notations. All these are separable as 'formal' elements; yet the conventions of real forms extend beyond them, with significant but not regular relations to them.

Thus the *presentation of persons* ('*characters*') has significantly variable conventions. Consider two standard variables in such presentation: personal appearance and social situation. Almost every conceivable combination of these elements, but also the exclusion of one or even both, has been conventionally practised in drama and narrative, Moreover, within each, there is a significant conventional range: from briefly typical presentation to exhaustive analysis. Further, the conventional variations in the presentation of 'personal appearance' correspond to deep variations in the effective perception and valuation of others, often in close relation to variations in the effective significance of family (lineage), social status, and social history, which are variable contexts of the essential definition of presented individuals. The difference of presentation between the undelineated medieval Everyman and the nineteenth-century fictional character whose appearance, history, and situation are described in sustained significant detail is an obvious example. What may be less obvious is the kind of absence, ratified by convention, in literature nearer our own time, where the conventions may appear to be not 'literary' or indeed not conventions at all, but self-defining criteria of significance and relevance. Thus the inclusion or exclusion of specific family or social history, or indeed of any detailed identity 'before the event', represents basic conventions of the nature of individuals and their relationships.

The selection of individuals, presented in any of these ways, is again evidently conventional. There is hierarchical selection by status, as in the old limitation of tragic status to persons of rank, a convention consciously discarded in bourgeois tragedy. In modern class societies the selection of characters almost always indicates an assumed or conscious class position. The conventions of selection are more intricate when hierarchy is less formal. Without formal ratification, all other persons may be conventionally presented as instrumental (servants, drivers, waiters), as merely environmental (other people in the street), or indeed as essentially absent (not seen, not relevant). Any such presentation depends on the acceptance of its convention, but it is always more than a 'literary' or 'aesthetic' decision. The social hierarchy or social norms that are assumed or invoked are substantial terms of relationship which the conventions are intended (often, in the confidence of a form, not consciously) to carry. They are no less terms of social relationship when the hierarchy or selection is not manifestly social but is based on the assignment of different orders of significant being to the selected few and the irrelevant many. Gogol's satirical account of this fundamental problem of the writer of modern internal consciousness—where, if the problem is taken literally, nobody can move without contact with another being whose internal consciousness demands similar priority and who will therefore cancel the chosen first person singular—highlights the selective internal convention through which this problem is temporarily solved, though beyond the convention the basic issue of significance of being remains.

Other conventions control the specification of such matters as work or income. In certain presentations these are crucial, and in all relationships they are evidently available facts. The convention which allows them to be treated as unimportant, or indeed to be absent, in the interest of what is taken as primary identity or an alternatively significant social character, is as evidently general as that less common but still important converse convention through which people are specified only at the level of general social and economic facts, with no individuation beyond them.

Significant facts of real relationships are thus included or excluded, assumed or described, analysed or emphasized by variable conventions which can be identified by formal analysis but can be understood only by social analysis. Variable conventions of *narrative stance* (from 'omniscience' to the necessarily limited 'personal' account) interact with these conventions of selection and exclusion in very complex ways. They interact also with significant conventions of the *wholeness of an account*, which involve radical questions of the nature of events. Certain stories require, conventionally, a pre-history and a projected ('after' or 'ever after') history, if their reading of cause, motive, and consequence is to be understood. The exclusion of such elements, like their inclusion, is not an 'aesthetic' choice—the 'way to tell a story'—but a variable convention involving radical social assumptions of causation and consequence. (Compare the final 'settlement' chapter in early Victorian English novels—e.g. Gaskell's *Mary Barton*—and the final 'breakaway' chapter in English novels between 1910 and 1940—e.g. Lawrence's *Sons and Lovers*.) Similarly, variable conventions of temporal sequence, while serving other ends—altered perceptions of event and memory, for example—interlock with these basic assumptions of causation and consequence, and thus with the conventional processes through which these are understood and the conventional criteria of relevant evidence.

Again, the presentation of *place* depends on variable conventions from a deliberate unlocation to a simple naming to a brief sketch to variably detailed description, up to the point where, as it is said, the place itself becomes a 'character' or 'the character'. Radically variable assumptions of the relations between people and places, and between 'man' and 'nature', are conveyed in these apparently self-evident ways. Other conventions assume or indicate variable relations between places and societies—'environments'—over a range from the abstraction of place from people, through the perception of people as symptoms of places, to the active apprehension of places as made by people. Descriptions of great houses, of rural landscapes, of cities, or of factories are evident examples of these variable conventions, where the 'point of view' may be experienced as an 'aesthetic' choice but where any point of view, including that which excludes persons or converts them into landscape, is social.

There are similar conventions for the description of *action*. Variations in direct and indirect presentation, and of focus within direct presentation, are especially marked in three kinds of human action: killing, the sexual act, and work. It is often said that these are matters of taste and fashion. But in each case the convention adopted assumes a specific (if often complex) relation of the event to other events and to more general organizations of significance. Thus violent death is 'central' in Greek tragedy, yet it is never presented but is reported or subsequently displayed. Other presentations are relatively formal, within speech or song, or within formal situations which are intended to define the act. At another extreme the detail of the event is predominant. It is not a question of abstract 'appropriateness'. It is often a question of whether the killing is significant primarily in its motivation or consequence, or whether these are secondary or irrelevant to the event and to the intended experience of the event itself. (Compare descriptions of the corpse in detective stories, where the convention indicates the occasion for an investigation and no more—in a context of rational control rather than of general or metaphysical reference—yet where a contradictory convention, a bloody immediacy, is often employed. As in all cases of confused or overlapping conventions, there is ground here for an investigation of problems of consciousness which cannot be reduced to the abstract methods of a particular kind of story.) Again, changing levels of description of sexual intercourse and of its preliminaries and variants involve general conventions of social discourse and its inclusions and exclusions, but also specific conventions which follow from variable relations of the act to changing institutions and relationships. Thus specific conventions of 'subjective' experience (the act as experienced by one partner with the other conventionally excluded; the act as consumed; the act as verbalized for pseudo-consumption) can be contrasted with conventions within which the act is habitual or even indifferent, abstracted, distanced, or merely summarized or implied in concentration on its 'objective' social effect. The variable levels of physical description can be interestingly compared with the variable levels of the description of work. There is a similar range of 'subjective' and 'objective' conventions, from work as experienced in physical or other detail to work as a simple indicator of social position. Of course in much of our received literature an earlier convention had operated, the persons chosen being relieved from the necessity to work at all, in the class-situation that corresponds to their selection as interesting. Thus, at a more overt level than in the case of sexuality, the distinction is not only between abstract 'subjective' and 'objective' viewpoints. The conventions rest, ultimately, on variations in the perception of work as an agent or condition of general consciousness, and thus, not only in work but in sexuality and in public action, on radically variable assumptions of human nature and identity: assumptions that are usually not argued but, through literary conventions, presented as 'natural' or self-evident.

A range of conventions in the presentation of speech has been closely studied, especially by the formalists (and it is significant that speech has received more attention than character, action, or place). There has been important analysis of the formal modes of presentation, representation, direct and indirect report, and reproduction. The relation between the styles of narrative and of directly represented speech is especially important in fictional conventions. One significant social distinction is between an integrity of style, based on a real or assumed social identity between narrator and characters (as in Jane Austen), through various hierarchical differentiations, to the break or even formal contrast between narrated and spoken language (as in George Eliot or Hardy). Conventional orthographies of variation, for foreign or regional speech, and crucially, in bourgeois literature, as class indications, are local examples of a range which establishes overt or, as often, displaced and covert social relationships which, except in these 'isolable' forms, are usually not seen as parts of the substantial human composition.

There is important variation between historical periods in the range of available conventions. Some periods have comparatively few; others, like our own, have comparatively many and permit substantial variations, themselves ultimately related to different real positions and formations. In certain periods of relative stability the conventions are themselves stable and may be seen as no more than formal, the 'rules' of a particular art. In other periods the variation and indeed uncertainty of conventions have to be related to changes, divisions, and conflicts in the society, all normally going deeper (beyond what are still, in certain privileged areas, taken as 'rules' or as neutrally variable aesthetic methods) than can be seen without analysis. For it is of the essence of a convention that it ratifies an assumption or a point of view, so that the work can be made and received. The modern controversy about conventions, or the cases of deliberate exposure or reversal of older or inherent conventions in an attempt to create new relations with audiences, thus relate directly to the whole social process, in its living flux and contestation. But the reality of conventions as the mode of junction of social position and literary practice remains central. It is then necessary to consider the relation of conventions, over the range indicated, to the concepts of genre and of form.

6. Genres

The most sustained attempt to group and organize the multiplicity of notations and conventions, evident in actual writing, into specific modes of literary practice is the theory of genres or kinds. This theory has an immense history. It is present in a particular form in Aristotle, where 'species' of poetry are defined in terms of a 'generic' definition of the art of poetry as such. It is a central issue in the complex intellectual conflicts of the Renaissance and its consequences. It is again a central issue in the complex modern conflicts between different kinds of theory and different kinds of empiricism.

It is important first to identify one level of the problem which has been the ground of much of the best reported argument and yet which is intellectually relatively trivial. This is the opposition between a theory of fixed genres, which was the neoclassical form of the more complex classifications of Greek and Renaissance thought, and an answering empiricism, which demonstrated the impossibility or inefficacy of reducing all actual and possible literary works to these fixed genres. In this reduced and peripheral argument, we are hardly faced with genre-theory at all, but with conflicting versions of practice put forward by distinct and opposed cultural formations. One formation based itself firmly on past practice, on what it abstracted as the 'standards' of 'classical' literature. This emerged in its most influential and weakest form as the definition of 'rules' for each 'genre', illustrated from existing works, prescribed for new works. It is significant but marginal that many of these rules did not have even the 'classical' authority they claimed. The formation belonged to feudalism and post-feudalism in decline, and the definitions have a related formal rigidity, in idealization of past practice, which can be shown—as in the notorious case of the rules of 'unity' in drama—to fit badly or even to contradict the practice on which they appeared to rely. Some empirical reply was therefore inevitable, but the substantial history was not at this level. What really defeated this residual form of genre-theory was the powerful and irresistible development of new kinds of work, which did not fit the classifications or follow the 'rules'. New classifications and new rules could of course be devised, but in developing bourgeois society the dominant impulse was not of this kind. Genre theory, in its most familiar abstract forms, was replaced by theories of individual creativity, of innovative genius, and of the movement of the individual imagination beyond the restricted and restricting forms of the past. We can compare this with the defeat and replacement of a social theory of 'estates', with fixed rules and functions, by a social theory of self-realization, individual development, and the mobility of primary forces. The changes in literary theory, and to a lesser extent in literary practice, came later than the changes in social practice and theory, but the correspondences are evident and significant.

Yet, just as bourgeois social theory did not end in individual liberalism but in new practical definitions of *classes* of individuals (*class* replacing *estate* and *order* in uneven and complex ways but with a necessary new stress on inherent flexibility and mobility), so bourgeois literary theory did not end in theories of individual creativity and genius. As in the related case of individual liberalism, these were not abandoned but they were practically supplemented. Genre and kind lost their neo-classical abstraction and generality, and lost also their senses of specific regulation. But new kinds of grouping and classification, of an empirical and relativist tendency, became habitual. Indeed these carried, in new ways, prescriptive elements, in modes of critical response and by implication in actual production.

Thus a novel is a work of creative imagination and the creative imagination finds its appropriate form, but there are still things a novel 'can' or 'cannot' do: not as a matter of rules but as a matter of the now specialized characteristics of the 'form'. (The novel 'cannot', for example, include unmediated ideas, 'because' its proper subject-matter is 'individuals' and their relationships.) At the same time, within these more general groupings, the variety of practice was recognized, in a limited way, by the proliferation of 'genres' and 'sub-genres' of a new kind: not the formal generalizations of epic, lyric, and dramatic, but (to quote from a current encyclopaedia) "novel, picaresque novel, romance, short-story, comedy, tragedy, melodrama, children's literature, essay, humour, journalism, light verse, mystery and detective stories, oratory, parody, pastoral, proverb, riddle, satire, science fiction". To be sure this is the reduction of classification to absurdity. But it is, in its own way, the debris of this kind of empiricism, representing as it does the combination of at least three types of classification: by literary form, by subject-matter, and by intended readership (this last a developing type in terms of specialized market-sectors), to say nothing of classifications which are combinations of these or which represent late, desperate entries to include some miscellaneous but popular type.

Strictly, of course, this is not genre theory at all. But it has the strengths as well as the weaknesses of this kind of empiricism. It is concerned with practical differences in real production, and with the discovery of some indicative bearings within the sheer vastness of production. As such, it is a more significant response than the residual imposition of abstract categories, as in a revived neo-classicism. It is not more ridiculous to discern local and transient empirical categories, such as the 'comedy thriller' or the 'metaphysical Western', than to classify nineteenth and twentieth-century novels, *a priori*, as variants of 'epic' or 'romance'. The former tendency represents a rootless but also a restless empiricism; the latter, ordinarily, a decayed idealism, directed by 'essential' and 'permanent' categories which have lost even their metaphysical status and become technical, seeing all practice as variants of already established 'ideal' forms. The single merit of the latter is that, unlike the former, it provokes, even as it displaces, certain necessary general questions.

The relation of Marxism to a theory of genres is subject to these variations of tendency. We face again the familiar problem of a complex relation between open social and historical analysis, which includes social and historical analysis of the received categories, and that 'transformation of idealism', in post-Hegelian tendencies, which retains the categories in (presumably) altered forms. Thus some Marxist accounts of genre retain an academic categorization, to which they add, in an epochal dimension, social and historical notes and 'explanations'. Other, more Hegelian accounts, as in Lukács, define genres in terms of their intrinsic relations to 'totality'. This leads to important insights but does not overcome the problem of the mobility of the category of totality between an ideal (non-alienated) state and an empirical (but then also differentiated) social whole. For any adequate social theory, the question is defined by the recognition of two facts: first, that there are clear social and historical relations between particular literary forms and the societies and periods in which they were originated or practised; second, that there are undoubted continuities of literary forms through and beyond the societies and periods to which they have such relations. In genre theory, everything depends on the character and process of such continuities.

We can distinguish, first, between nominal continuity and substantial continuity. 'Tragedy' for example, has been written, if intermittently and unevenly, in what can appear to be a clear line between fifth-century B.C. Athens and the present day. A relevant factor of this continuity is that authors and others described successive works as 'tragedies'. But to assume that this is a simple case of the continuity of a 'genre' is unhelpful. It leads either to abstract categorization of a supposed single essence, reducing or overriding the extraordinary variations which the name 'tragedy' holds together; or to definitions of 'true tragedy', 'mixed tragedy', 'false tragedy', and so on, which cancel the continuity. This way of defining genre is a familiar case of giving category priority over substance.

'Genre' has in fact, until recently, been a term of classification which has brought together, and then often confused, several different kinds of generic description. Renaissance theory, defining 'species' and 'modes' within a general theory of 'kinds', was much more particular but was, on the other hand, insufficiently historical. It was indeed to cope with historical combinations of different levels of organization that the looser concept of 'genre' was adopted. But, in its later stages especially, this single advantage was surrendered and genre-theory was left with largely abstract and diverse collocations.

It is necessary, first, to break these up into their basic components, which are:(i) *stance*; (ii) *mode of formal composition*; (iii) *appropriate subject-matter*. 'Stance' was traditionally defined in the three categories of the narrative, the dramatic, and the lyrical. These can no longer serve but they indicate the dimension that is in question: a mode of basic (social) organization which determines a particular kind of presentation—the telling of a story, the presentation of an action through characters, univocal expression, and so on. These can be reasonably taken as general and distinct (though at times in practice associated) forms of composition and address. Their socio-cultural and historical extent is very wide indeed. Many cultures and periods include work over this whole range of possible stances, and significant social and historical variation, at this level, is largely or wholly a matter of degree. 'Mode of formal composition' is very much more variable: each of any of the possible stances can be linked with one or more specific kinds of writing: verse or prose, particular forms of verse, and so on. Real social and historical content is frequently evident in these particular linkages, but certain kinds of technical solution to persistent problems of composition can last beyond their original periods: in some specific cases (particular verse forms; particular narrative devices) and in many more general cases (the tenses of narrative, for example, or the procedure of recognition in drama). 'Appropriate subject-matter' is more variable again. Linkages between a stance and/or a mode of formal composition and either the scope (selected social, historical or metaphysical reference) or the quality (heroism, suffering, vitality, amusement) of any particular subject-matter are, while sometimes persistent (often residually persistent), especially subject to social, cultural, and historical variation.

It is therefore impossible, in any historical theory, to combine these different levels of organization into *definitive* forms. Their actual combinations are of irreducible historical importance, and must be always empirically recognized. But any *theory* of genre must from the beginning distinguish between them. Is such a theory necessary? It can seem that historical analysis of specific linkages, and of their specific connections with more general formations and forms of organization, is in itself sufficient. Certainly it is work that still largely remains to be done, in adequate ways, over a sufficient number of examples. Yet it remains true that even this analysis requires recognition of the full range of variables which compose specific organizations. The profound and often determining variables of stance, for example, are especially likely to be overlooked, or to be given insufficient weight, in local historical analysis. Moreover, if we are to attempt to understand writing as historical practice in the social material process, we have to look again, beyond traditional generic theory, at the whole question of determinants. Modern formalist theory, beginning at the level of modes of formal composition, returned these to questions of stance which it could then interpret only in terms of permanent variables. This led straight to idealism: archetypal dispositions of the human mind or condition. Sociological theory, on the other hand, beginning at the level of subject-matter, derived formal composition and stance from this level alone: at times convincingly, for the choice of subject-matter includes real determinants, but still in general insufficiently, for what has finally to be recognized is that stance, especially, is a social relationship, given a particular form of socio-cultural organization, and that modes of formal composition, over the range from traditional to innovatory, are necessarily forms of a social language.

Genre-classification, and theories to support various types of classification, can indeed be left to academic and formalist studies. But recognition and investigation of the complex relations between these different forms of the social material process, including relations between processes at each of these levels in different arts and in forms of work, are necessarily part of any Marxist theory. Genre, in this view, is neither an ideal type nor a traditional order nor a set of technical rules. It is in the practical and variable combination and even fusion of what are, in abstraction, different levels of the social material process that what we have known as genre becomes a new kind of constitutive evidence.

7. Forms

In the most substantial literary theory of the last two centuries, genre has in practice been replaced by form. Yet the concept of form contains a significant ambiguity. From its development in Latin, which was repeated in English, it acquired two major senses: a visible or outward shape, and an inherent shaping impulse. Form thus spans a whole range from the external and superficial to the essential and determining. This range is evidently, if not always consciously, repeated in literary theory. At its extremes it is found in neo-classical and academic theories, stressing external characteristics and evident rules by which forms can be distinguished and in which particular works may be found to be perfect or imperfect; and then in romantic theories, in which form is regarded as the unique and specific achievement of a particular vital impulse, all external characteristics and indeed all rules being regarded as irrelevant, at best a mere crust on the dynamic internal formative impulse. It is an advantage of this range of theories that we can all see works to which one or other is relatively appropriate: works in which a form is faithfully followed, rules carefully observed, and other works in which an eventually discernible form appears to be quite unprecedented, a unique shaping from a particular experience. This recognition makes for an easy eclecticism, but leaves the real theoretical problems of form quite untouched. For as so often, the range and ambiguity of a concept, far from being an invitation to mere listing, or an eclectic tolerance, constitute the key to its significance. We have seen this already in the concepts of *culture* and of *determination*. The case of *form* is a perhaps even more striking example.

We can begin by agreeing that the characteristics to which each kind of theory draws attention—the defining importance of available forms on the one hand, and the crucial insistence on the active making of forms on the other—are indeed the truths of practice. What is really significant is the complex relation between these truths. It is this relation which the contrasting theories in their ordinary terms evade. The evasion is significant because it repeats certain other structurally comparable evasions, which in the course of time have become habitual: the firmly held but practically and logically incompatible categories of 'the individual' and 'society' are a closely related case. Thinking which begins from such categories, and then moves to the construction of theories of value around one or other projected pole, fails to give adequate recognition to the constantly interactive and in this sense dialectical process, which is real practice. Any categorical product of this process is at most a relative and temporary stabilization: a recognition of degree which is often important in itself but which needs always to be returned to the originating whole process if it is to be fully understood even in its own terms.

Thus neo-classical theories of form, usually expressed in some version of genre theory, unquestionably recognize and describe certain artistic forms, and even correctly identify their rules, while at the same time limiting understanding both of the forms and of the status of these 'rules' by failure to recognize that the forms were made, the rules arrived at, by a long and active process of active shaping, of trial and error, which can be described in the terms of the opposite theory, as an internal shaping impulse. Again, Romantic theories of form unquestionably recognize and describe the processes of the discovery of certain forms, under the pressures of experience and practice, but then fail to recognize, within their stress on uniqueness, the quite general new forms which emerge. Neo-classical theories hypostasize history, while Romantic theories reduce it to a flux of moments.

For a social theory of literature, the problem of form is a problem of the relations between social (collective) modes and individual projects. For a social and historical theory, it is a problem of these relations as necessarily variable. For a social and historical theory based on the materiality of language and the related materiality of cultural production, it is a problem of the description of these variable relations within specifiable material practices.

Thus a social theory can show that form is inevitably a relationship. Form depends, that is to say, on its perception as well as its creation. Like every other communicative element, from the most local to the most general, it is always in this sense a social process which, in those conditions of extension of the continuity on which the process itself is absolutely dependent, becomes a social product. Forms are thus the common property, to be sure with differences of degree, of writers and audiences or readers, before any communicative composition can occur. This is much easier to recognize in the case of stable traditional forms, where a specific relationship, of a collective or relatively general kind, is called upon and activated in the very processes of composition and performance. In such cases the two processes are often significantly close and at times even indistinguishable. It is impossible to overestimate the significance which is then felt and shared. The hearing of certain traditional arrangements of words; the recognition and activation of certain rhythms; the perception, often through already shared themes, of certain basic flows and relations and in this deep sense real compositions, real performances: all these are parts of some of our most profound cultural experiences. In their accessible forms they are of course made and remade within specific cultural traditions, which may indeed be extended and borrowed. In some of their basic forms, which are obviously difficult to separate from the shared accessible forms, they may well relate to certain shared 'physical' and 'mental'—active—life processes of evolved human organization.

It is clear that these more recognizable sharings of form are at the more collective end of any social continuum. It is understandable that one kind of Marxism puts great stress on this collective reality, and sees in it the origin of art of all kinds. This is often continued with polemics against 'individualistic' art, which have the consequence of making most modern work and modern theory (and not only bourgeois work and bourgeois theory) theoretically inaccessible. It is often also combined with arbitrary deductions of this basic social process from a separated 'original' work process (see the discussion of productive forces on p. 94). But it is clear that the collective mode which can sustain and contain all individual projects is only one of a number of possible relationships. Individual variations on such basically collective forms as heroic stories, 'romances', and 'myths' are almost always possible. Individual variations on shared and already-known dramatic forms are widely evident, and the effects of such variations, precisely in their relation to certain expected forms—for example, the conscious variation of rhythm or the departure from an expected ending—still belong to the shared primary process, the effect of the variation depending on recognition both of the expected form and of the change.

These intermediate cases account for a relatively large part of composition, especially as we trace the development of properly collective forms, related to whole communities, to more specific group forms, often related to a social class, in which the same formal qualities of shared recognition and activation, and within these shared variation, are evident.

But there are cases beyond these. There are the significant cases which have preoccupied Romantic and post-Romantic theory, in which form is not already shared and available, and in which new work is something much more than variation. Here still, undoubtedly, new *forms* are created, often drawing on very basic elements of the activation of recognition and response but in ways that do not, at first or for a long time, cohere in a manner that can be readily shared. In these cases the creation of forms is undoubtedly also a relationship, but one that is different in kind from its opposite extreme of wholly shared and stable repeatable forms. As in the case of language, new formal possibilities, which are inherently possibilities of a newly shared perception, recognition, and consciousness, are offered, tested, and in many but not in all cases accepted. It is indeed commonplace to observe of this type that later generations find no difficulty with a form, now shared, that was once virtually inaccessible and indeed widely seen as formless.

This range of the variable relationships inherent in forms takes on a different aspect when we add a historical dimension. It is clear that there are significant correlations between the relative stability of forms, institutions, and social systems generally. Most stable forms, of the kind properly recognizable as collective, belong to social systems which can also be characterized as relatively collective and stable. Most mobile, innovative, and experimental forms belong to social systems in which these new characteristics are evident or even dominant. Periods of major transition between social systems are commonly marked by the emergence of radically new forms, which eventually settle in and come to be shared. In such periods of major and indeed minor transition it is common to find, as in the case of genres, apparent continuations or even conscious revivals of older forms, which yet, when they are really looked at, can be seen to be new. Greek choral tragic drama (itself marked by significant internal development and variation in its own 'classical' period) has at different times been widely imitated and even consciously revived, but never reproduced. Two results of this process, classical opera and neo-classical tragedy, show this historical dynamic very clearly, and the subsequent internal development, at least of the former, actively exemplifies the process of relative innovation and relative stabilization. On the other hand the new form of the novel, radical variation as it is on older forms of prose romance and history, has throughout its development been mobile, innovative, and experimental, defying all attempts to reduce it to a 'form' of an older, more stable, and more collective kind. The radically new form of contemporary prose drama, from the seventeenth century, has shown profound innovation, variation, and internal development, with consequent periods of stabilization and of experiments beyond the stabilization, in ways characteristic of both formal and historical practice in a developing society. *There is thus no abstract theoretical relationship between collective modes and individual projects. The degree of distance between them, within the continuing reality of each mode of consciousness, is historically variable as a function of real social relationships, both general and specific.*

These modes of consciousness are material. Every element of form has an active material basis. It is easy to see this in the 'materials' of forms: words, sounds, and notations, as in speech and writing; other physically produced elements in other arts. But it is always more difficult to see certain essential properties of form—properties of relation, in a wide sense—in material ways. It is especially difficult when 'matter' and 'consciousness' are disjoined, as in idealism or in mechanical materialism. For the truly *formative* process is not the passive disposition of material elements. Indeed this is often recognized in (sometimes accurate) description of certain dispositions as 'random'. What is at issue in form is the activation of specific relations, between men and men and between men and things. This can be recognized, as it often is in modern theory, but then distanced into an abstraction of rhythm, or proportion, or even 'symbolic form'. What these abstractions indicate are real processes but always physical and material relational processes. This is as true of the most 'subjective' generative moments—the poem first 'heard' as a rhythm without words, the dramatic scene first 'visualized' as a specific movement or grouping, the narrative sequence first 'grasped' as a moving shape inside the body—as of the most 'objective' moments—the interaction of possible words with an already shared and established rhythm, the plasticity of an event 'taking shape' in its adaptation to a known form, the selection and reworking of sequence to reproduce an expected narrative order.

This whole range of conscious, half-conscious, and often apparently instinctive shaping—in an intricate complex of already materialized and materializing forms—is the activation of a social semiotic and communicative process, more deliberate, more complex, and more subtle in literary creation than in everyday expression but in continuity with it through a major area of direct (specifically addressed) speech and writing. Over this whole range, from the most indifferent adoption of an established relational linguistic form to the most worked and reworked newly possible form, the ultimately formative moment is the material articulation, the activation and generation of shared sounds and words.

The formalists were then right to give priority to the specific material articulation which is a literary work. But they were wrong to specialize this emphasis to 'literary language'. They were right to explore the articulation in concrete ways, as in the doctrine of specific 'devices'. But it is not necessary to limit the analysis of articulation to the important idea of 'dominants', which determine specific organizations. Such dominants are often evident (the single hero, for example, in Renaissance tragedy), but other kinds of organization show more complex relations of leading or stressed elements which do not so much subordinate other elements as define them (the inheritance plot in the nineteenth-century novel, for example, often in complex relations with the discovery of identity through new relationships). The formalist emphasis on the 'device' as 'estranging' (making strange) is a correct observation of one kind of art, in a period of restless and necessary experiment against fixed (hegemonic) forms, but it cannot be extended to a principle of form as such: the materializing of *recognition* is an evident formal element of much of the great art of the world. Yet it is in this kind of attention to precise material articulations—in which and only in which specific consciousness, specific feeling, is realized—that the true social practice and analysis of art must begin.

8. Authors

From several angles, within a social perspective, the figure of the author becomes problematic. To see individuation as a social process is to set limits to the isolation but also perhaps to the autonomy of the individual author. To see form as formative has a similar effect. The familiar question in literary history, 'what did this author do to this form?' is often reversed, becoming 'what did this form do to this author?'. Meanwhile, within these questions, there is the difficult general problem of the nature of the active 'subject'.

The word 'author', much more than 'writer' or 'poet' or 'dramatist' or 'novelist', carries a specific sense of an answer to these questions. It is true that it is now most often used as a convenient general term, to cover writers of different kinds. But in its root and in some of its surviving associations it carries a sense of decisive origination, rather than simply, as in 'writer' or in the more specific terms, a description of an activity. Its most general early uses included a regular reference to God or Christ, as the authors of man's condition, and its continuing association with 'authority' is significant. Its literary use, in medieval and Renaissance thought, was closely connected with a sense of 'authors' as 'authorities': the 'classical' writers and their texts. In the modern period there is an observable relation between the idea of an author and the idea of 'literary property': notably in the organization of authors to protect their work, by copyright and similar means, within a bourgeois market.

Two tendencies in Marxist thought bear on these questions. There is the well-known emphasis on the changing social situation of the writer. In its most accessible form this points to such changes as that from patronage to the bookselling market: a significant, complicated, and continuing history, But this history of changing conditions can be seen as a second-order problem: how the author *distributes* his work. The more interesting indication takes the active social relationships one or more stages back, showing first the effect of demand on what is viably produced, under patronage or within a particular market; and second the more internal effects—the specific pressures and limits—within actual composition. The evidence for both kinds of effect is extensive, and can never reasonably be overlooked. But even where it is fully admitted, the idea of the author, in all but its most romantic forms, is essentially untouched. The author has 'his' work to do, but he finds difficulties in getting it supported or sold, or he cannot do it exactly as he would have wished, because of the pressures and limits of the social relationships on which, as a producer, he depends. This is, in the simplest sense, the political economy of writing: a necessary addition to any real history of literature, but still no more than an addition.

The second tendency transforms the whole problem. It points to the figure of the individual author, as to the related figure of the individual subject, as a characteristic form of bourgeois thought. No man is the author of himself, in the absolute sense which these descriptions imply. As a physical individual he is of course specific, though within a determining genetic inheritance. As a social individual he is also specific, but within the social forms of his time and place. The crucial argument then turns on the nature of this specificity and these forms, and on the relations between them. In the case of the writer one of these social forms is central: his language. To be a writer in English is to be already socially specified. But the argument moves beyond this: at one level to an emphasis on socially inherited forms, in the generic sense; at another level to an emphasis on socially inherited and still active notations and conventions; at a final level to an emphasis on a continuing process in which not only the forms but the contents of consciousness are socially produced. The ordinary figure of the author can be made compatible with the first two levels. This is the language, these are the forms, these are the notations and conventions, on which he fundamentally depends but from which, still, he begins to be an author. It is only at the final level that what seems to be the keep of the concept—his individual autonomy—is radically attacked or overrun.

Many people react sharply when this point in the argument is reached. Even its theoretical expression is quickly connected with administrative measures against authors, with authoritarian directives and with actual censorship and suppression, and this is not always gratuitous. The weakness of the bourgeois concept of 'the author', as of 'the individual', is its naïvety, which in its own ways, and especially in the market, can become in practice cruel and malign. Any version of individual autonomy which fails to recognize, or which radically displaces, the social conditions inherent in any practical individuality, but which has then, at another level, to reintroduce these social conditions as the decisive 'practical business' of the everyday world, can lead at best to self-contradiction, at worst to hypocrisy or despair. It can become complicit with a process which rejects, deforms, or actually destroys individuals in the very name of individualism. Yet the concept has, correspondingly, a certain strength. Within its explicit limits it is well placed to defend one sense of individual autonomy against certain forms of the social which have become themselves deformed. In the central tradition of Marxism the separated concepts of 'individual' and 'society' are radically unified, but reciprocally and indeed dialectically:

It is above all necessary to avoid postulating 'society' once more as an abstraction confronting the individual. The individual is a *social being*. The manifestation of his life—even when it does not appear directly in the form of a social manifestation, accomplished in association with other men—is therefore a manifestation of *social life* . . . Though man is a *unique* individual—and it is just his particularity which makes him an individual, a really *individual* social being—he is equally the *whole*, the ideal whole, the subjective existence of society as thought and experienced. (*EPM*, 105)

Yet in some versions and applications of the Marxist tradition, this reciprocal and dialectical relationship has been deformed. The 'social', we might say, has been deformed to the 'collective', just as, in the bourgeois tradition, the 'individual' has been deformed to the 'private'. There are real practical dangers in both, and any Marxist thinking has to face the fact that a society claiming its authority has made the theoretical deformation into an appalling practice, in just this area of the relation between writers and their society. Again, beyond this chilling area of practice, there is a more modern theoretical tendency (the Marxist variant of structuralism) in which the living and reciprocal relationships of the individual and the social have been suppressed in the interest of an abstract model of determinate social structures and their 'carriers'. Facing either the practice or this version of the theory, it is not surprising that many people run back headlong into bourgeois-individualist concepts, forms, and institutions, which they see as their only protection.

It is then necessary to look for more adequate and more precise theoretical positions. (More precise since some elements even of Marx's definition, for example 'the ideal whole', are unsatisfactory, and seem indeed to be residual from earlier, non-materialist, forms of thought.) It must be said, first, that recognition of all the levels of sociality—from the external forms of the political economy of literature, through the inherited forms of genres, notations, and conventions, to the constitutive forms of the social production of consciousness—is inevitable. But it is at the level of the constitutive that precision is especially necessary. The most interesting contribution is Goldmann's analysis (1970, 94–120) of the 'collective subject'. It is a difficult term, and we must first define its distinction from other uses of 'collective'. Goldmann was careful to distinguish it from Romantic ideas of the 'absolute collective' (of which the Jungian 'collective unconscious' is a modern example), in relation to which the individual is merely an epiphenomenon. He distinguished it also from what we can call the 'relative collective' of Durkheim, where collective consciousness is situated 'outside, above, or alongside' individual consciousness. What is actually being defined is not so much a 'collective' as a 'trans-individual' subject, in two senses.

There is the relatively simple case of cultural creation by two or more individuals who are in active relations with each other, and whose work cannot be reduced to the mere sum of their separate individual contributions. This is so common in cultural history, in cases where it is clear that something new happens in the very process of conscious co-operation, that it does not seem to present any serious difficulties. But it is from just this realization of a relatively well-known experience that the second and more difficult sense of a collective subject is developed. This goes beyond conscious co-operation—collaboration—to effective social relations in which, even while individual projects are being pursued, what is being drawn on is trans-individual, not only in the sense of shared (initial) forms and experiences, but in the specifically creative sense of new responses and formation. This is obviously more difficult to find evidence for, but the practical question is whether the alternative hypothesis of categorically separate or isolated authors is compatible with the quite evident creation, in particular places and at particular times, of specific new forms and structures of feeling. Of course when these are identified they are still 'only' forms and structures. Individual works range from what seem perfect examples of these forms and structures, through convincing or suggestive instances, to significant and sometimes decisive variations. Any procedure which shortens this range is merely reductive: the 'collective' becomes absolute or external. But on the other hand it is often the case, when we consider the whole work of individual authors, and especially when we consider it as an active development in time, that different elements of the range seem to apply more or less closely in different phases.

It is then an open question whether the significant relation, at any one point, is with the 'trans-individual' form or structure, or with the abstracted individual. Or, to put it another way, the 'development' of an author can be (subsequently) summarized as separate, to be related only when it is complete to other complete and separate 'developments'. Alternatively, this very process of development can be grasped as a complex of active relations, within which the emergence of an individual project, and the real history of other contemporary projects and of the developing forms and structures, are continuously and substantially interactive. This latter procedure is the most significant element in modern Marxist accounts of cultural creation, as distinct both from the better-known Marxist version in which an author is the 'representative' of a class or tendency or situation, to which he can then be substantially reduced, and from bourgeois cultural history in which, against a 'background' of shared facts, ideas, and influences, every individual (or in its more common bourgeois form, every *significant* individual) creates his quite separate work, to be subsequently compared with other separate lives and works.

The character of the problem can be clearly seen in one literary form: the biography. It is a common experience when reading the biography of a selected individual, in a given time and place, to see not only his individual development but a more general development in which, within the conventions of the form, other people and events form round him and in this crucial sense are defined by him. This is a relatively satisfactory reading experience until we read other biographies of the same time and place, and realize the displacements of interest, perspective, and relation which we must now be conscious of, but which, with that first biography, we had almost unwittingly taken as natural.

The momentary minor figure is now the very centre of interest; the key events appear and disappear; the decisive relationships shift. We are not likely then willingly to go back to some general account in which all these emphatic identities are merged into an 'impersonal' class or group. But neither can we stay as we are, with a mere miscellaneity or even contradiction of identities. Slowly, and reaching beyond the very edges of the form, we can gain the real sense of living individuals in every kind of relationship and in certain significantly common situations, and we come to know that we cannot understand their whole lives simply by adding each life to the other. At this point we begin to see the relations—not only the interpersonal but also the truly social—within which (but not necessarily subject to which) the distinguishable identities and phases of identity developed.

This procedure can be summarized as a reciprocal discovery of the truly social in the individual, and the truly individual in the social. In the significant case of authorship it leads to dynamic senses of social formation, of individual development, and of cultural creation, which have to be seen as in radical relationship without any categorical or procedural assumption of priorities. Taken together, these senses allow a fully constitutive definition of authorship, and its specification is then an open question: that is to say, a set of specific historical questions, which will give different kinds of answer in different actual situations.

This is my only difference, on this point, from Goldmann, who, following Lukács's distinction of 'actual' and 'possible' consciousness, sees great writers as those who integrate a vision at the level of the possible ('complete') consciousness of a social formation, while most writers reproduce the contents of ('incomplete') actual consciousness. This can be true, and such a theory has the advantage that integration can be relatively simply demonstrated at the level of form. But it need not always be true, for it includes a very classical presupposition. The real relations of the individual, the trans-individual, and the social may include radical tension and disturbance, even actual and irresolvable contradictions of a conscious kind, as often as they include integration. Abstracted notions of integral form must not be used to override this.

Moreover we have necessarily to be concerned with cultural creation as a whole, and not only with the significant cases of the homology of formation and (ideal) form. Indeed any procedure which categorically excludes the specificity of all individuals and the formative relevance of all real relations, by whatever formula of assigned significance, is in the end reductive. We do not have to look for special cases to prove a theory. The theory that matters, in the known and irreducible variations of history, is that realization of the socially constitutive which allows us to see specific authorship in its true range: from the genuinely reproductive (in which the formation is the author), through the wholly or partly articulative (in which the authors are the formation), to the no less important cases of the relatively distanced articulation or innovation (often related to residual or emergent or pre-emergent formations) in which creativity may be relatively separated, or indeed may occur at the farthest end of that living continuum between the fully formed class or group and the active individual project. In this at once social and historical perspective, the abstract figure of 'the author' is then returned to these varying *and in principle variable* situations, relationships, and responses.

9. Alignment and Commitment

Our intense and continuing argument about the relations of writers to society often takes the form of an argument about what is variously called 'alignment' or 'commitment'. But it is soon apparent, in this argument, that several different questions are being discussed, and that some confusion is caused by radical variations in what 'alignment' and 'commitment' are taken to be.

It is a central proposition of Marxism, whether expressed in the formula of base and superstructure or in the alternative idea of a socially constituted consciousness, that writing, like other practices, is in an important sense always aligned: that is to say, that it variously expresses, explicitly or implicitly, specifically selected experience from a specific point of view. There is of course room for argument about the precise nature of such a 'point of view'. It does not, for example, have to be detachable from a work, as in the older notion of a 'message'. It does not have to be specifically political, or even social in the narrowest sense. It does not, finally, have to be seen as in principle separable from any specific composition. Yet these qualifications are not meant to weaken the original claim, but simply to clarify it. Alignment in this sense is no more than a recognition of specific men in specific (and in Marxist terms class) relations to specific situations and experiences. Of course such a recognition is crucial, against the claims to 'objectivity', 'neutrality', 'simple fidelity to the truth', which we must recognize as the ratifying formulas of those who offer their own senses and procedures as universal.

But if all writing is in this sense aligned, what is the point, at any time, of a demand for commitment? Is not this always a demand to write from one point of view rather than from others, and in this sense a demand for affiliation, conversion, or even obedience? Protests against this demand have been often enough made by the enemies of Marxism, who suppose, falsely, that only Marxism and its associated movements ever make it. Let another protest be entered, from a Marxist: Brecht against Lukács and his Moscow colleagues in the 1930s:

They are, to put it bluntly, enemies of production. Production makes them uncomfortable. You never know where you are with production;

production is unforeseeable. You never know what's going to come out. And they themselves don't want to produce. They want to play the *apparatchik* and exercise control over other people. Every one of their criticisms contains a threat. (Quoted in W. Benjamin, 'Talking to Brecht', *New Left Review*, 77, 55)

This is a real protest, in a real situation, in which, in the name of socialism, many writers were cajoled, repressed, and even destroyed. Yet it is also simply one example of the innumerable protests of many writers in many periods, against the actual or would-be controllers of production, in Church, State, or market.

But has this practical or theoretical pressure on writers anything to do, necessarily, with 'commitment'? Commitment, if it means anything, is surely conscious, active, and open: a choice of position. Any idea can be abused, by a self-referring and controlling authority. 'Freedom to publish', for example, can be practically redefined as 'freedom to publish at a profit'. The key question, in the matter of alignment and commitment, is the nature of the transition from historical analysis, where every kind of alignment and every kind of commitment can be seen in actual writing, to contemporary practice, where all the alignments and commitments are in active question. The latter, evidently, is disturbing. Many positions can be tolerated when they are dead. A safe Marxism sticks to historical analysis and in its adaptation in academic studies shows every sign of doing so. But the central thrust of Marxism is the connection of theory and practice. How does this actually work through, in the case not only of commitment but of the apparently less controversial alignment?

Marx and Engels said several hard things against 'tendency literature':

It became more and more the habit, particularly of the inferior sorts of *literati*, to make up for the want of cleverness in their productions by political allusions which were sure to attract attention. Poetry, novels, reviews, the drama, every literary production teemed with what was called 'tendency'. (Engels, October 1851; cit. *MEL*, 119)

. . . a worthless fellow who, due to lack of talent, has gone to extremes with tendentious junk to show his convictions, but it is really in order to gain an audience. (Engels, August 1881; cit. *MEL*, 123)

But these comments, leaving aside their characteristic aggressiveness, relate to what might be called 'applied tendency'—the mere addition of political opinions and phrases, or unrelated moral comments, of the kind Marx found in Eugene Sue, among "the most wretched offal of socialist literature" (*The Holy Family*, 1845, cit. MEL, 119). The case is different with the profound social and historical critique and analysis which they praised in other writers, whether it was implicit, as in Balzac, or explicit, as in what Marx called "the present splendid brotherhood of fiction writers in England". He instanced Dickens and Thackeray, Miss Brontë and Mrs. Gaskell,

whose graphic and eloquent pages have issued to the world more political and social truths than have been uttered by all the professional politicians, publicists and moralists put together. (*The English Middle Class*, 184, cit. MEL, 105)

Marx and Engels's discussions of Lassalle's play *Franz von Sickingen* (MEL, 105–11) stressed the need for a profound understanding of social and historical crisis, as against reduced or simplifying treatments. But that such an understanding is 'aesthetically' necessary, and that it is radically connected with social and historical (including political) understanding, is never doubted for a moment. Indeed the critique of 'tendency literature' is not a case against 'commitment' but a case for serious commitment: the commitment to social reality.

The controversy about commitment could not, of course, remain at this general level. It became active, in several different social and historical situations, when commitment became practical and even programmatic. Thus Sartre's arguments for commitment, in the specific conditions of post-war Europe, rested on a belief in its inevitability:

If literature is not everything, it is worth nothing. This is what I mean by 'commitment'. It wilts if it is reduced to innocence, or to songs. If a written sentence does not reverberate at every level of man and society, then it makes no sense. What is the literature of an epoch but the epoch appropriated by its literature? (*The Purposes of Writing*, 1960; in Sartre (1974), 13–14)

Writers, necessarily involved with meanings, "reveal, demonstrate, represent; after that, people can look at each other face to face, and act as they want" (ibid, 25). Sartre was arguing against notions of 'pure art', which when they are serious are always forms (however concealed) of social commitment, and which when they are trivial are simple evasions. At the same time he complicated this position by an artificial distinction between poetry and prose, reserving the inevitability of commitment to the 'meanings' of the prose-writer and seeing meaning and emotion in the poem as transformed into 'things', beyond this dimension. Adorno's critique of this position is convincing. The artificial separation of prose reduces writing, beyond the reserved area of poetry, to a conceptual status, and leaves all questions of commitment *in writing* unanswered. (It is of course an aspect of Sartre's commitment to freedom that they are left unanswered). Moreover, within this general definition, as Adorno further argued, "commitment . . . remains politically polyvalent so long as it is not reduced to propaganda". *

These are the flexible formulations and qualifications of one style of Marxist thought, relatively close, in spirit, to what Marx and Engels incidentally indicated. The harder questions, and with them the harder formulations, arose in direct relation to open revolutionary practice: in the Russian revolution and again in the Chinese revolution. Both Lenin and Trotsky saw writers, with other artists, as necessarily free to work in their own ways: "to create freely according to his ideals, independent of anything" (Lenin, *Collected Works* (1960), iv, 2, 114); "to allow . . . complete freedom of self-determination in the field of art" (Trotsky, *Literature and Revolution*, 242). But each made reservations; Lenin on the cultural policy of the Revolution, which could not "let chaos develop in any direction it may", Trotsky making self-determination subject to "the categorical standard of being for or against the Revolution". It was from the reservations, and not from the assertions, that one version of 'commitment' became practical and powerful, extending from the level of general cultural policy to specification of the form and content of 'committed' or 'socialist' (the terms now in practice interchangeable) writing. What was then written was not all, or not merely, 'tendency literature', but the most public form of the argument was of that kind: 'commitment' as political affiliation, in a narrowing series of definitions (often polemically and administratively fused): from the cause of humanity to the cause of the people to the revolution to the party to the (shifting) party line.

The crisis thus provoked in Marxist thought is still evidently unresolved. It was useful, after such an experience, to find Mao

* 'Commitment', *New Left Review*, 1974, 87–8.

Tse-Tung saying: "it is harmful to the growth of art and science if administrative measures are used to impose one particular style of art and school of thought and to ban another" (Mao Tse-Tung (1960), 137). But this was not a return to liberalism; it was an insistence on the reality of open struggle, between new and old forms of consciousness and new and old kinds of work. It was again subject to a reservation: "as far as unmistakable counter-revolutionaries and wreckers of the socialist cause are concerned, the matter is easy: we simply deprive them of their freedom of speech" (ibid, 141). But this, at least at first, did not imply any doctrinaire equivalence between writing in a revolutionary society and any specific style: "Marxism includes realism in artistic and literary creation, but cannot replace it" (Ibid, 117). Instead there is an emphasis on creative impulses "rooted in the people and the proletariat", and a corresponding opposition to creative impulses arising from other classes and ideologies. This, it must be remembered, is a definition of the work of *socialist* writers.

In the complexities of practice, formulations of this kind can be developed in very different directions. But what is theoretically most interesting in Mao's argument, alongside previously familiar positions, is an emphasis on the transformation of social relations between writers and the people. This can be reduced to the familiar emphasis on certain kinds of content and style, but it has also been developed in ways that change the whole problem. 'Commitment' is a move by a hitherto separated, socially and politically distanced, or alienated writing. Mao's alternative theoretical and practical emphasis is on *integration*: not only the integration of writers into popular life, but a move beyond the idea of the specialist writer to new kinds of popular, including collaborative, writing. The complexities of practice are again severe, but at least theoretically this is the germ of a radical restatement.

Most earlier discussions of commitment are either in effect a variant of formalism (an abstract definition or imposition of a 'socialist' style) or a late version of Romanticism, in which a writer commits himself (as man and writer, or with nuances between these) to a cause. The more significant Marxist position is a recognition of the radical and inevitable connection between a writer's real social relations (considered not only 'individually' but in terms of the general social relations of 'writing' in a specific society and period, and within these the social relations embodied in particular kinds of writing) and the 'style' or 'forms' or 'content' of his work, now considered not abstractly but as expressions of these relations. This recognition is power-less if it is in itself abstract and static. Social relations are not only received; they are also made and can be transformed. But to the decisive extent that they are *social* relations there are certain real pressures and limits—genuine determinations—within which the scope of commitment as individual action and ges-ture must be defined.

Commitment, strictly, is conscious alignment, or conscious change of alignment. Yet in the material social practice of writ-ing, as in any other practice, what can be done and attempted is necessarily subject to existing or discoverable real relations. Social reality can amend, displace, or deform any merely intended practice, and within this (at times tragically, at times in ways which lead to cynicism or active disgust) 'commitment' can function as little more than an ideology. Conscious 'ideo-logy' and 'tendency', supporting each other, must then often be seen as symptoms of specific social relationships and failures of relationship. Thus the most interesting Marxist position, because of its emphasis on practice, is that which defines the pressing and limiting conditions within which, at any time, specific kinds of writing can be done, and which correspond-ingly emphasizes the necessary relations involved in writing of other kinds. The Chinese ideas of integration with the people, or of moving beyond the exclusiveness of the specialist writer, are mere slogans unless the transformed social practice on which such ideas must depend is genuinely active. They are not, that is to say, in their most serious forms, simple and abstract ideologi-cal positions. In any specific society, in a specific phase, writers can discover in their writing the realities of their social relations, and in this sense their alignment. If they determine to change these, the reality of the whole social process is at once in ques-tion, and the writer within a revolution is necessarily in a differ-ent position from the writer under fascism or inside capitalism, or in exile.

This does not or need not mean that a writer postpones or abandons his writing until some desired change has happened. Nor should it mean that he becomes resigned to the situation as he finds it. Yet all practice is still specific, and in the most serious and genuinely committed writing, in which the writer's whole being, and thus, necessarily, his real social existence, is inevitably being drawn upon, at every level from the most manifest to the most intangible, it is literally inconceivable that practice can be separated from situation. Since all situations are dynamic, such practice is always active and is capable of radical development. Yet as we have seen, real social relations are deeply embedded within the practice of writing itself, as well as in the relations within which writing is read. To write in different ways is to live in different ways. It is also to be read in different ways, in different relations, and often by different people. This area of possibility, and thence of choice, is specific, not abstract, and commitment in its only important sense is specific in just these terms. It is specific within a writer's actual and possible social relations as one kind of producer. It is specific also in the most concrete forms of these same actual and possible relations, in actual and possible notations, conventions, forms and language. Thus to recognize alignment is to learn, if we choose, the hard and total specificities of commitment.

10. Creative Practice

At the very centre of Marxism is an extraordinary emphasis on human creativity and self-creation. Extraordinary because most of the systems with which it contends stress the derivation of most human activity from an external cause: from God, from an abstracted Nature or human nature, from permanent instinctual systems, or from an animal inheritance. The notion of self-creation, extended to civil society and to language by pre-Marxist thinkers, was radically extended by Marxism to the basic work processes and thence to a deeply (creatively) altered physical world and a self-created humanity.

The notion of creativity, decisively extended to art and thought by Renaissance thinkers, should then, indeed, have a specific affinity with Marxism. In fact, throughout the development of Marxism, this has been a radically difficult area, which we have been trying to clarify. It is not only that some important variants of Marxism have moved in opposite directions, reducing creative practice to representation, reflection, or ideology. It is also that Marxism in general has continued to share, in an abstract way, an undifferentiated and in that form metaphysical celebration of creativity, even alongside these practical reductions. It has thus never finally succeeded in making creativity specific, in the full social and historical material process.

The loose use of 'creative' to describe any and every kind of practice within the artificial grouping (and mutual self-definition) of 'the arts' and 'aesthetic intentions' masks these difficulties, for others as well as for Marxists. It is clear that the radical differences and differentials of these highly variable specific practices and intentions have to be described and distinguished if the terms are to acquire any real content. Most of even the best discussions of 'Art' and 'the Aesthetic' rely to an extraordinary extent on predicated selection, yielding conveniently selective answers. We have to refuse the short cut so often proposed, by which the 'truly creative' is distinguished from other kinds and examples of practice by a (traditional) appeal to its 'timeless permanence' or, on the other hand, by its affiliation, conscious or demonstrable, with 'the progressive development of humanity' or 'the rich future of man'. Any such proposition might eventually be verified. But to know, substantially, even a little of what such phrases point to, in the extraordinary intricacies and variations of real human self-creation, is to see the phrases themselves, in their ordinary contexts, as abstract gestures, even where they are not, as they have so often been, mere rhetorical cover for some demonstrably local and temporary value or injunction. If the whole vast process of creation and self-creation is what it is said, abstractly, to be, it has to be known and felt, from the beginning, in less abstract and arbitrary and in more concerned, more regarding, more specific, and more practically convincing ways.

To be 'creative', to 'create', means many quite evidently different things. We can consider one central example, where a writer is said to 'create' characters in a play or a novel. At the simplest level this is obviously a kind of production. Through specific notations, and using specific conventions, a 'person' of this special kind is made to 'exist'—a person whom we may then feel we know as well as, or better than, living persons of our acquaintance. In a simple sense something has then been created: in fact the means of notation to know a 'person' through words. All the real complexities then at once follow. The person may have been 'copied' from life, in as full and accurate a verbal 'transcription' as possible of a living or once living person. The 'creation' is then the finding of verbal 'equivalence' to what was (and in some cases could still alternatively be) direct experience. It is far from clear, however, that this 'creative' practice, taken only so far, differs in any significant way, except perhaps in its limitations, from meeting and knowing someone. The point is often made that this 'creative' practice enables us to get to know interesting people whom we could not otherwise have met, or more interesting people than we could ever hope to meet. But then this, though in many circumstances important, is a kind of social extension, privileged accessibility, rather than 'creation'. Indeed, 'creation' of this kind seems to be no more than the creation of (real or apparent) opportunities.

It is interesting to see how far this point might extend beyond the simple and in fact relatively rare cases of a person 'copied from life'. Most such 'transcriptions' are necessarily simplifications, by the sheer fact of selection if by nothing else (the most uneventful life would take a library of books to transcribe). More common cases are 'copying' certain aspects of a person: physical appearance, social situation, significant experiences and events, ways of talking and behaving. These are then projected into imagined situations, following an element of the known person. Or aspects of one person may be combined with aspects of one or more others, into a new 'character'. Aspects of a person may be separated and counterposed, rendering an internal relationship or conflict as a relation or conflict between two or more persons (the known person, in such a case, may well be the writer). Are these processes 'creative', beyond the simple sense of verbal production?

Not by definition, it would seem. It is only as the processes of combination, separation, projection (and even transcription) become processes beyond the bare production of characters that their description as 'creative' becomes plausible. There is the case, so often recorded, of a writer beginning with some known or observed person, whom he works to reproduce, only to find, at a certain stage of the process, that something else is happening: something usually described as the character 'finding a will (a life) of his own'. What is then in fact happening? Is it taking the full weight, perceived as an 'external' substance, of any human understanding, even in the simplest sense of recording another life? Is it coming to know the full weight of imagined or projected relations? It seems to be a highly variable active process. It is often interpreted, while it lasts, not as 'creating' but as contact, often humble, with some other ('external') source of knowledge. This is often mystically described. I would myself describe it as a consequence of the inherent materiality (and thence objectified sociality) of language.

It cannot be assumed that, even allowing for the complexities, the normal 'creative' process is the movement away from 'known' persons. On the contrary, it is at least as common for a character to be 'created' from other (literary) characters, or from known social types. Even where there are other real starting-points, this is usually what happens, eventually, in the great majority of plays and novels. And then in what sense are these processes 'creation'? In fact all these modes have an essential similarity, since the 'creation' of characters depends on the literary conventions of characterization. But there are evident differences of degree. In most drama and fiction the characters are already pre-formed, as functions of certain kinds of situation and action. 'Creation' of characters is then in effect a kind of tagging: name, sex, occupation, physical type. In many important plays and novels, within certain class modes, the tagging is still evident, at least for 'minor' characters, according to social conventions of distribution of significance (the 'characterization' of servants, for example). Even in more substantial characterization, the process is often the activation of a known model. But then it must not be supposed that individuation is the sole intention of characterization (though tension or fracture between that retained intention and the selective use of models is significant). Over a wide range of intentions, the real literary process is *active reproduction*. This is especially clear within dominant hegemonic modes, and in residual modes. The 'persons' are 'created' to show that people are 'like this' and their relations 'like this'. The method can range from crude reproduction of an (ideological) model to intent embodiment of a convinced model. Neither is 'creation' in the popular sense, but the range of real processes, from illustration and different levels of typification to what is in effect *performance* of a model, is significant.

The detailed and substantial *performance of a known model* of 'people like this, relations like this', is in fact the real achievement of most serious novels and plays. Yet there is evidently also a mode beyond reproductive performance. There can be new articulations, new formations of 'character' and 'relationship', and these are normally marked by the introduction of different essential notations and conventions, extending beyond these specific elements to a total composition. Many of these new articulations and formations become, in their turn, models. But while they are being formed they are creative in the emergent sense, as distinct from the senses of 'creative' which are ordinarily appropriated for the range from reproduction to performance.

The creative in this emergent sense is comparatively rare. It is necessarily involved with changes in social formation, but two qualifications are necessary. First, that these are not necessarily, and certain not only directly, changes in institutions. The social area excluded by certain practical hegemonies is often one of their sources. Secondly, that the emergent is not necesssarily the 'progressive'. For example, the character as inert object, reduced to a set of failing physical functions, as in late Beckett, can be construed as 'alienated' and linked to a social—in fact deliberately excluded—model. Yet the typification is not only articulative but communicative. In imitation especially the new type is offered to convince, and incorporation begins.

Literary production, then, is 'creative', not in the ideological sense of 'new vision', which takes a small part for the whole, but in the material social sense of a specific practice of self-making, which is in this sense socially neutral: self-composition. It is the particular function of a social theory to understand the range of processes within this general practice. We have to make clear specific distinctions between their many examples, over and above the alternative specialized descriptions which limit, control, and would often exclude these decisive distinctions. In the vital area of contemporary social practice there can be no reserved areas. Nor is it only a matter of analysis and description of alignment. It is a matter of recognizing the issues as parts of a whole social process which, as it is lived, is not only process but is an active history, made up of the realities of formation and of struggle.

The sharpest realization of this active history, a realization which brings with it at once the inevitabilities and the necessities of social and political action, must include realization of the variable realities of this practice, which are so often put under pressure or, from deformed or false theory, relegated to the secondary or the marginal, displaced as the superstructural, distrusted as apparently independent production, even controlled or silenced by injunctions. To see the full social dimension of this kind of production is to take it more seriously, and more seriously *as itself*, than has been possible in more specialized political or aesthetic perspectives. Every mode in its range, from reproduction and illustration through embodiment and performance to new articulation and formation, is a crucial element of practical consciousness. Its specific means, so powerfully developed and practised, are wholly indispensable: the capacity to reproduce and to illustrate, at what seems the lower end of the range; the capacity to embody and perform, a profound activation of what may be known but in these ways is radically known, in detail and in substance; and then the rare capacity to articulate and to form, to make latencies actual and momentary insights permanent. What we generalize as art is often, within a social theory, recognized and honoured from its original collective functions. It needs even more real respect—a respect of principle—in all its subsequently more varied functions, in complex societies and in the still more complex societies which real socialism envisages.

For creativity relates, finally, to much more than its local and variable means. Inseparable as it always is from the material social process, it ranges over very different forms and intentions which, in partial theories, are separated and specialized. It is inherent in the relatively simple and direct practice of everyday communication, since the signifying process itself is always, by its nature, active: at once the ground of all that is social and the renewed and renewable practice of experienced and changing situations and relationships. It is inherent in what is often distinguished from it as self-composition, social composition, often dismissed as ideology, for these also are always active processes, dependent on specific immediate and renewable forms. It is inherent most evidently, but not exclusively, in new articulations and especially in those which, given material durability, reach beyond their time and occasion.

Writing is so central a material social art that it has of course been used, and continues to be used, in all these forms and intentions. What we find is a true continuum, corresponding to the at once ordinary and extraordinary process of human creativity and self-creation in all its modes and means. And we have then to reach beyond the specialized theories and procedures which divide the continuum. Writing is always communication but it cannot always be reduced to simple communication: the passing of messages between known persons. Writing is always in some sense self-composition and social composition, but it cannot always be reduced to its precipitate in personality or ideology, and even where it is so reduced it has still to be seen as active. Bourgeois literature is indeed bourgeois literature, but it is not a block or type; it is an immense and varied practical consciousness, at every level from crude reproduction to permanently important articulation and formation. Similarly the practical consciousness, in such forms, of an alternative society can never be reduced to a general block of the same dismissive or celebratory kind. Writing is often a new articulation and in effect a new formation, extending beyond its own modes. But to separate this as art, which in practice includes, always partly and sometimes wholly, elements elsewhere in the continuum, is to lose contact with the substantive creative process and then to idealize it; to put it above or below the social, when it is in fact the social in one of its most distinctive, durable, and total forms.

Creative practice is thus of many kinds. It is already, and actively, our practical consciousness. When it becomes struggle—the active struggle for new consciousness through new relationships that is the ineradicable emphasis of the Marxist sense of self-creation—it can take many forms. It can be the long and difficult remaking of an inherited (determined) practical consciousness: a process often described as development but in practice a struggle at the roots of the mind—not casting off an ideology, or learning phrases about it, but confronting a hegemony in the fibres of the self and in the hard practical substance of effective and continuing relationships. It can be more evident practice: the reproduction and illustration of hitherto excluded and subordinated models; the embodiment and performance of known but excluded and subordinated experiences and relationships; the articulation and formation of latent, momentary, and newly possible consciousness.

Within real pressures and limits, such practice is always difficult and often uneven. It is the special function of theory, in exploring and defining the nature and the variation of practice, to develop a general consciousness within what is repeatedly experienced as a special and often relatively isolated consciousness. For creativity and social self-creation are both known and unknown events, and it is still from grasping the known that the unknown—the next step, the next work—is conceived.

Booklist and Abbreviations

ABBREVIATIONS USED IN THE TEXT

CCP   Marx, *A Contribution to the Critique of Political Economy*
EPM   Marx, *Economic and Philosophical Manuscripts of 1844*
GI   Marx and Engels, *The German Ideology*
MEL   Marx and Engels on Literature and Art, ed. Baxandall and
       Morawski
SW   Marx and Engels, *Selected Works*

BOOKLIST

(All editions in English where available)

ADORNO, T., *Prisms*, London, 1967.
—— *Negative Dialectics*, London, 1973.
ALTHUSSER, L., *For Marx*, London, 1969.
—— and BALIBAR, E. *Reading Capital*, London, 1970
ANDERSON, P., 'Components of the National Culture', *New Left Review*,
    50, London, 1968.
AUERBACH, E., *Mimesis*, Princeton, 1970.
BAKHTIN, M., *Rabelais and his World*, Cambridge, Mass., 1968.
BARTHES, R., *Writing Degree Zero*, London, 1967.
—— *Mythologies*, New York, 1972.
BAXANDALL, S., *Marxism and Aesthetics: a selective annotated bibliog-*
    raphy, New York, 1968.
—— (ed.) *Radical Perspectives in the Arts*, Baltimore, 1972.
—— and MORAWSKI, S. (ed.), *Marx and Engels on Literature and Art*
    (MEL), St. Louis, 1973.
BENJAMIN, W., *Illuminations*, New York, 1966.
—— *Understanding Brecht*, London, 1973.
—— *Charles Baudelaire*, London, 1973.
BERGER, J., *Toward Reality: Essays in Seeing*, New York, 1962.
BLOCH, E., *On Karl Marx*, New York, 1971.
BRECHT, B., *On Theatre* (ed. Willett, J.), New York, 1964.
BUKHARIN, N., *Historical Materialism*. London, 1965.
CAUDWELL, C., *Studies in a dying Culture*, London, 1938.
—— *Illusion and Reality*, London, 1938.
—— *Further Studies in a Dying Culture*, London, 1949.
CAUTE, D., *The Fellow Travellers*, New York, 1972.
COLLETTI, L., *From Rousseau to Lenin*, London, 1973.
—— *Marxism and Hegel*, London, 1974.
DAY-LEWIS, C. (ed.), *The Mind in Chains*, London, 1937.
DELLA VOLPE, G., *Critica del Gusto*, Milan, 1960.

DEMETZ, P., *Marx, Engels and the Poets*, Chicago, 1967.

DUNCAN, H. D., *Annotated Bibliography on the Sociology of Literature*, Chicago, 1947.

DUVIGNAUD, J., *The Sociology of Art*, London, 1972.

EAGLETON, T., *Exiles and Émigrés*, London, 1971.

ECO U., *Apocalittici e Integrati*, Milan, 1968.

EHRMANN, J. (ed.), *Literature and Revolution*, Boston, 1967.

ENGELS, F., *Dühring's Revolution in Science*, Moscow, 1954.

—— *Condition of the Working Class in England, 1844*, London, 1892.

—— *Ludwig Feuerbach*, London, 1933.

ENZENZBERGER, H. M., 'Constituents of a Theory of the Media', *New Left Review* 64, London, 1970.

FAN, L. H. (ed.), *The Chinese Cultural Revolution*, New York, 1968.

FEKETE, J., "A Theoretical Critique of Some Aspects of North American Critical Theory', (Ph.D., Cambridge, 1972).

FIORI, G., *Antonio Gramsci*, London, 1970.

FISCHER, E., *The Necessity of Art*, London, 1963.

—— *Art Against Ideology*, New York, 1969.

FLORES, A. (ed.), *Literature and Marxism*, New York, 1938.

FOX, R., *The Novel and the People*, London, 1937.

GARAUDY, R., *Marxism in the Twentieth Century*, New York, 1970.

GOLDMANN, L., *The Hidden God*, London, 1964.

—— *The Human Sciences and Philosophy*, London, 1969.

—— *Marxisme et sciences humaines*, Paris, 1970.

——*Towards a Sociology of the Novel*, London, 1975.

GORKY, M., *On Literature*, Moscow, 1960.

GRAMSCI, A., *Modern Prince and Other Writings*, London, 1957.

—— *Prison Notebooks*, London, 1970.

GUILLEN, C., *Literature as System*, Princeton, 1971.

HALL, S., and WHANNEL, P., *The Popular Arts*, London, 1964.

HAUSER, A., *The Social History of Art*, New York, 1957.

HEATH, S. C., *The Nouveau Roman*, London, 1972.

HENDERSON, P., *Literature and a Changing Civilisation*, London, 1935.

HOGGART, R., *The Uses of Literacy*, London, 1957.

—— *Speaking to Each Other*, London, 1970

HORKHEIMER, M., *Critical Theory*, New York, 1972.

—— and ADORNO, T. *Dialectic of Enlightenment*, London, 1973.

HOWARD, D., and KLARE, K. (ed.), *The Unknown Dimension: European Marxism since Lenin*, New York, 1972.

JACKSON, T. A., *Charles Dickens*, London, 1937.

JAMESON, F., *Marxism and Form*, Princeton, 1972.

—— *The Prison House of Language*, Princeton, 1972.

JAY, M., *The Dialectical Imagination*, London, 1973.

KETTLE, A., *Introduction to the English Novel*, London, 1955.

KLINGENDER, F., *Art and the Industrial Revolution*, London, 1947.

KORSCH, K., *Marxism and Philosophy*, London, 1972

KRISTEVA, J., *Semeiotike*, Paris, 1969.

LABRIOLA, A., *The Materialistic Conception of History*, Chicago, 1908.

LANG, B., and WILLIAMS, F., *Marxism and Art*, New York, 1972.

LAURENSON, D. T., and SWINGEWOOD, A., *The Sociology of Literature*, London, 1972.

LEAVIS, F. R. (ed.), *Towards Standards of Criticism*, London, 1933.

—— *The Common Pursuit*, London, 1952.

LENIN, V. I., *Selected Works*, London, 1969.

—— *On Literature and Art*, Moscow, 1967.

LENNEBERG, E. H., *Biological Foundations of Language*, New York, 1967.

LICHTHEIM, G., *Marxism: A Historical and Critical Study*, London, 1961.

LIFSHITZ, M., *The Philosophy of Art of Karl Marx*, New York, 1938.

LINDSAY, J., *After the Thirties*, London, 1956.

LOWENTHAL, L., *Literature and the Image of Man*, Boston, 1957.

LUKÁCS, G., *The Historical Novel*, London, 1962.

—— *Studies in European Realism*, London, 1950.

—— *The Meaning of Contemporary Realism*, London, 1962.

—— *The Theory of the Novel*, London, 1971.

—— *History and Class Consciousness*, London, 1971.

MACHEREY, P., *Pour une théorie de la production littéraire*, Paris, 1970.

MAO TSE-TUNG, *On Literature and Art*, Peking, 1960.

MARKOVIC, M., *The Contemporary Marx*, London, 1974.

MARCUSE, H., *One-Dimensional Man*, Boston, 1964.

—— *Negations*, Boston, 1969.

—— *The Philosophy of Aesthetics*, New York, 1972.

MARX, K., *Capital*, London, 1889.

——*A Contribution to the Critique of Political Economy* (CCP), London, 1909.

—— *Economic and Philosophic Manuscripts of 1844* (EPM), Moscow, 1961.

—— *Essential Writings* (ed. Caute, D.), London, 1967.

—— *Grundrisse*, London, 1973.

—— *Selected Writings* (ed. Bottomore, T. B., and Rubel, M), London, 1963.

—— and Engels, F., *The Communist Manifesto*, London, 1888.

—— —— *The German Ideology* (GI), London, 1963.

—— —— *Selected Works* (SW), 2 vols., London, 1962.

MATLAW, R. E. (ed.), *Belinsky, Chernyshevsky and Dobrolyubov*, New York, 1962.

MAYAKOVSKY, V., *How are Verses Made?*, London, 1970.

MESZAROS, I. (ed.), *Aspects of History and Class Consciousness*, London, 1971.

Modern Quarterly, vol. 2, London 1946–7 and vol. 6, London 1951.

MORAWSKI, S., *Inquiries into the Fundamentals of Aesthetics*, London, 1974.

MORRIS, W., *On Art and Socialism*, London, 1947

MOZHNYAGUN, S. (ed.), *Problems of Modern Aesthetics*, Moscow, 1969.

Mukarovsky, J., *Aesthetic Function, Norm and Value as Social Facts*, Ann Arbor 1970.

New Left Review, London, 1960– .

North, J. (ed.), *New Masses.*, New York, 1972.

Orwell, G., *Critical Essays, Journalism and Letters*, London, 1968.

Plekhanov, G., *Critical Essays in the History of Materialism*, London, 1934.

—— *Art and Social Life*. London, 1953.

Raskin, J., *The Mythology of Imperialism*, New York, 1971.

Revai, J., *Literature and People's Democracy*, New York, 1950.

Richards, I. A., *Principles of Literary Criticism*, London, 1924.

Rockwell, J., *Fact in Fiction*, London, 1974.

Rossi-Landi, F., *Semiotica e Ideologia*, Milan, 1972.

—— *Language as Work and Exchange*, The Hague, 1975.

Rubel, M., *Bibliographie des oeuvres de Karl Marx*, Paris, 1956.

Sartre, J–P., *Search for a Method*, New York, 1963.

—— *What is Literature?*, New York, 1966.

—— *Between Existentialism and Marxism*, London, 1974.

—— *Critique of Dialectical Reason*, London, 1976.

Saussure, F. de, *Cours de Linguistique Générale*, Lausanne, 1916.

Schiller, H. I., *Mass Communications and American Empire*, New York, 1970.

Schlauch, M. *Language*, New York, 1967.

Schneierson, A. (ed.), *Fundamentals of Dialectical Materialism*, Moscow, 1967.

Socialist Register, London, 1964– .

Solomon, M. (ed.), *Marxism and Art*, New York, 1973.

Stalin, J., *Marxism and Linguistics*, New York, 1951.

Thompson, E. P., *William Morris*, London, 1955.

—— *The Making of the English Working Class*, London, 1963.

Thomson, G., *Aeschylus and Athens*, London, 1941.

—— *Marxism and Poetry*, New York, 1946.

Timpanaro, S., *On Materialism*, London, 1976.

Todorov, T. (ed.), *Théorie de la littérature*, Paris, 1965.

Trotsky, L., *Literature and Revolution*, New York, 1957.

—— *On Literature and Art*, New York, 1970.

Vazquez, A. S., *Art and Society: essays in Marxist Aesthetics*, New York, 1973.

Vico, G., *The New Science*, tr. Bergin, T., and Fisch, M., Ithaca, N.Y., 1948.

Vološinov, V. N., *Marxism and the Philosophy of Language*, New York, 1973.

Vygotsky, L. S., *Thought and Language*, Cambridge, Mass., 1962.

—— *The Psychology of Art*, Cambridge, Mass., 1971.

West, A., *Crisis and Criticism*, London, 1937.

Williams, R., *The Long Revolution*, London, 1961.

—— *Television: Technology and Cultural Form*, London, 1974.

—— *Keywords*, London, 1976.

WILSON, E., *To the Finland Station*, New York, 1953.

ZHDANOV, A. A., *Essays on Literature, Philosophy and Music*, New York, 1950.

Index